Turning It Around

Redirectional Therapy

Also by Sidney M. Rosen, MSW, PhD and Deborah L.K. Spencer-Chun, MSW

Toward a Gang Solution: The Redirectional Method

Turning It Around

Redirectional Therapy

Sidney M. Rosen, MSW, PhD

Deborah L.K. Spencer-Chun, MSW

Adult Friends for Youth

VANTAGE PRESS
New York

Cover design by Victor Mingovits

Vantage Press and the Vantage Press colophon are registered trademarks of Vantage Press, Inc.

FIRST EDITION

Published by Vantage Press, Inc.
419 Park Ave. South, New York, NY 10016

Manufactured in the United States of America
ISBN: 978-0533-164905

Library of Congress Catalog Card No: 2011909428

0 9 8 7 6 5 4 3 2 1

To our young friends, who have taught us how to help them turn it around.

Contents

Acknowledgments

The staff of Adult Friends for Youth and their commitment to the philosophy and goals of AFY for twenty-five years have helped to deliver a new therapeutic approach for changing the behaviors of youth gangs and aggressive youths. Staff members have come and gone but their legacy lives on through those who have continued their work.

Two members of the present staff, Malakai (Mo) Maumalanga and Jane Castro Tampon, have been with AFY for over twenty years, both as clients and staff. Mo is an MSW and is AFY's clinical coordinator. Jane directs the annual fundraiser and the statewide Student Transition Convention for all students moving up from elementary to middle school. She is also AFY's office manager. Both have been invaluable to the agency's insight into youth problems and to its program development. Liz Yonamine works closely with Jane, lectures on drugs, and somehow managed to find time to type this manuscript, for which we are especially grateful.

Meja Kaniho trained as a redirectionalist with AFY and has been a mighty addition to the clinical program. She works closely with Deborah, Mo, and McKay Schwenke, AFY's Vice President and Senior Master Practitioner. Mac developed AFY's annual rugby tournament and has led the way in developing our mediation skills. Collectively, their day-to-day experience in the field validates Redirectional Therapy and provides new knowledge that enables this restless therapy to grow and become stronger. Hugs and kisses also to the Schwenke children, Telaviv, Kona, Seiko, Syrian, Hookela, and Vave and to McKay's wife Angie for many years of hard work and support, especially for their contributions to AFY's annual fundraiser and rugby tournament.

A special note of thanks goes to Terry Fisher, AFY's retired Chief Operating Officer, who persistently kept the clinical staff on track, mothered us all, and helped edit the manuscript.

We also recognize the invaluable contribution of Pasimi Hingano, our colleague, and co-author of AFY's first book, *Toward a Gang Solution; The Redirectional Method*, 1996, who provided us with a sociological perspective, went on to obtain his PhD, and now resides on the mainland.

Through two decades, Judie Rosen was the volunteer fundraising chairperson who made it possible for AFY to stay afloat financially. Deb is fond of noting that while Sid was the founder of AFY, Judie was the funder.

To Judie and Sean Chun (Deb's other half) and David, Marcella, Andrew and Ari Rosen; Corey, Lisa and Vivian (Vivi) Rosenlee; and Deb's mom Rosie and the Spencer family—we love you for appreciating the worth of what we believe we've needed to do and selflessly giving of yourselves to advance the work of AFY.

And, certainly not least, we greatly appreciate our many directors and board chairs, over a span of twenty-five years, who supported and encouraged our groundbreaking enterprise.

Sid Rosen, Founder and President Emeritus
Deborah L.K. Spencer-Chun, President and CEO
Adult Friends for Youth
Honolulu, Hawaii
March 18, 2011

Debbie Spencer, Our Angel

By Michael Quiaoit

Met her in the seventh grade
Beginning of a relationship that would never fade
Remember always giving schools the hardest time
If you scolded us, you would consider it a crime
For the craziest kids, you were always there
To ignore our cries for help, you would never dare
Even when we disappointed you, you still had the heart
Your memory inside all of us will never depart
Always treating us with the deepest respect
And always reminding us what's wrong and correct
Through all our problems, we could always count on you
When we had complications, picking up the phone was all we had to do
We wouldn't have made it if you weren't around
We always felt relief when we heard your voice's sound
I've learned so much from you and am eager to show it
Everything you've taught us when we were young suddenly hit
Now the thanks you properly earned
How so much from you... we've learned
Some of our hopes now follow your road
You've stopped our futures from becoming dark and cold
How you made all of Cross Sun and society's hands fit
Because of you, "We made it!"

Part I

The Method

Chapter 1

Introduction

Serendipity was the culprit that ensnared Adult Friends for Youth (AFY) into the world of youth gangs. AFY was a creature that emerged from a federal grant to the University of Hawaii School of Social Work in 1985. The two-year grant was, ostensibly, intended to demonstrate that volunteer mentors, working one on one with high-risk youths, could alter their risky behaviors and prevent subsequent incarcerations. The model was similar to the Big Brothers/Big Sisters approach, but with a population several years older and significantly more dangerous to others and to themselves.

As mentors undertook their work, it was not uncommon when they went to meet their "young friends" for them to find that they were often in the company of other youths. It was but a small leap to arrive at two basic realities. The first was that any meaningful impact on their behaviors could only be accomplished if their friends were involved, and the second was that the task of working with a group of high-risk youths was beyond the scope of volunteers. Concurrently, with the recognition that no meaningful change could occur outside of the group, came the awareness that these friendship groups were often youth gangs.

Before the grant was to terminate in 1987, AFY began to seek private funding that would allow it to continue as a private non-profit corporation beyond the grant period. It successfully accomplished this goal and changed its name, under the grant, from the Hawaii

Youth Services Volunteer Project to Adult Friends for Youth. It then began to focus on building a professional organization that could work with the youth gangs that it had encountered. The volunteer mentoring component of the new agency was significantly reduced in the early nineties and was discontinued in 1996.

By and large, youth gangs are perceived by both mental health professionals and the lay public as a law enforcement problem, whose members have crossed a line that makes them unresponsive to, and therefore unworthy of, having help offered to them. Society has turned them into pariahs to be controlled, not to be helped. What society has failed to comprehend is that contempt is a two-way, and, potentially, very destructive street. What it has also failed to appreciate is that there is a basic need by human beings to be valued and respected. One of our clients, Recky Cruz, in a poem that prefaced our earlier book (*Toward a Gang Solution*) said, "They treat us as if we ain't human, but inside our hearts there's a heart hard as diamond . . . the meaning for us lighted ones respect, respect everyone."

Efforts to see gang members as human beings and products of their environment are even ridiculed in song, e.g., "Gee, Officer Krupke," from *West Side Story*. One line that drips with sarcasm goes, "This boy don't need a judge, he needs an analyst's care!"

Ironically, while he may have been mocking "do-gooders" for their belief in the potential for therapeutic change, Stephen Sondheim actually almost got it right. One song that hits the environmental factor head-on is Elvis Presley's "In the Ghetto," written by Mac Davis. The idea that destructive violent behaviors can be changed therapeutically usually isn't a subject even open for discussion. In fact, Cloward and Ohlin (1960), positioned themselves in opposition to therapeutic intervention with gangs, and have had a major influence on social work thinking from the 1960s to the present day. Adult Friends for Youth is putting the concept of mental health intervention with this population back into play.

The National Resource Center for Youth Services at the University of Oklahoma, upon publishing AFY's book, *Toward a Gang Solution:*

The Redirectional Method, 1996, noted that the Redirectional Method is "a unique, field-tested, mental health approach to gangs and violent youths." In two decades of experience, AFY has found that Redirectional Therapy not only changes behaviors from destructive to constructive, but in so doing has created safer schools and healthier communities. AFY strongly advocates that it is far better, in the long run, not to simply protect students and teachers from bullies, who continue to be bullies, but to change the behavior of the bullies.

When we began working with gangs in 1989 the bleak expectations of many gang members was that they would end up in prison or die at a fairly young age. This fatalism, apparently, was often the reason for lack of interest in school and general hostility to the conventions of society. Illegal drugs and alcohol have been means of self-medicating to escape the pain of everyday life and indifference to life itself, which to many holds little value.

The high school graduation rate for gangs with whom we worked in 1990 was between 10–20 percent. In 1996, eighteen of the twenty-three members of the Junior Sons of Samoa graduated (78 percent) (Hingano, p. 74). Graduation rates for our clients have been consistently in the 70–80 percent range ever since. AFY, which also conducts an alternative high school diploma program for high-risk dropouts, under the auspices of the Hawaii Department of Education's Adult Education Competency-Based Education Program, has had, on average, a successful graduation rate of 80 percent, which jumped in 2007 to 91 percent. This exceeds the Hawaii public high school graduation rate, which, according to Complete College America, is 68 percent (Gima, *Star Bulletin*, 3/5/10). Testing and grading for AFY's program are tamper-proof, since they are conducted independently by the Department of Education. Therapeutic counseling wrapped around academics strongly influences the program's success.

Our experience has taught us that we have the knowledge to evolve youth gangs into nondestructive social groups, and by so doing break up gangs. We know that criminal and destructive behaviors can be changed into law-abiding and constructive behaviors, and that when provided with the opportunity this is what most gang members want for themselves. The problem, for the most part, has been the absence of a therapeutic mechanism that works on the street to help them change.

We have also found that, not infrequently, the OGs (Original Gangsters), adult gang members, also want a better life for the younger kids but see them trapped into the same lifestyle that had entrapped them. It may take time to earn the trust of the OGs, but more often than not, we've found that they see help as a good thing, and can be enlisted to support AFY's efforts.

AFY's relationship with law enforcement is interesting, to say the least. We've described it as constructive tension. Often we are advocating for the same youths that they see as the bad guys, whom they will intimidate and arrest if they can. However, over the years, recognition that we have a unique relationship that can defuse explosive situations has emerged. It is not unusual now, when confrontations are imminent, including gang-police confrontations, with helicopters hovering and the whole nine yards, that the police will permit AFY to move in and extract the youths who are involved. It is also not uncommon, even for youths who are not our clients, to respond favorably to AFY's staff members because of the agency's reputation.

AFY's unique role has gained a modest level of respect within law enforcement as it has become better understood. The job of educating the general public and the political community is an ongoing and uphill task, particularly with politicians who grow hair on their chests by showing how tough they are on crime.

Our successes have not gone unnoticed, and growing appreciation for a mental health approach to the gang problem has come from distinctly different quarters. Both the former U.S. Attorney in Hawaii, Ed Kubo, and the Hawaii Psychological Association (HPA), have acknowledged that AFY's therapeutic methodology works. In 2006 the HPA presented the agency with a specially created honor called the Po'okela Award for excellence in its work with a population that is outside the experience of most mental health professionals. HPA noted that the award was presented to AFY for promoting "educational achievement and offering a prescription of hope for significantly reducing poverty and destructive behaviors among gang members." Kubo stated, "AFY has been very instrumental in reducing the temptation for kids to become involved in gangs and it has also been very helpful to the Department of Education and the schools in preventing gang and youth violence." In 2008, Mental Health America of Hawaii presented AFY with the Outstanding Community Mental Health Agency Award "in recognition of more than two decades of service successfully helping to disband and rehabilitate youth gangs and provide support and preventive services to youths in at-risk situations and communities. Troubled youths know that they can depend on AFY never to give up on them, and we are honored to salute you for that commitment."

The Hawaii State Legislature also recognized AFY's work on the occasion of its Outstanding Agency Award presentation by "Commending and Honoring" it for its "therapeutic approach to the problems of high-risk youths (which) focuses on communities with high levels of critical youth issues, including drug use, unemployment, crime, poverty, gang involvement, teen pregnancy, and truancy, and establishing 'Redirectional Therapy (RT),' the cutting-edge mental health therapy for high-risk and gang youths in the United States."

We would welcome the opportunity to demonstrate, scientifically, that RT is effective with gang youths and other high-risk youths. However, since such a study would require a significant investment, it is unlikely to be funded anytime soon. Nevertheless, after twenty-five years, twenty-two of which have involved working with gangs, we have accumulated enough anecdotal evidence to demonstrate that we have been very successful in helping youths to free themselves from gangs and destructive lifestyles through the application of a replicable psychotherapeutic methodology.

Turning It Around will be presented in two parts. The first will present a group theory perspective of gangs, the philosophy and practice principles of Redirectional Therapy, and mediation. The second will explore RT's application through the stories of twelve AFY clients, and clinical practice with four gangs.

The approach that we call Redirectional Therapy is a replicable, nondirective, nonjudgmental therapy that has changed antisocial gang attitudes and behaviors into law-abiding constructive behaviors. We have found that as gang members become increasingly aware of their individual competencies, the cohesiveness of the group declines, and, correspondingly, independence increases.

AFY works with youth gangs as whole entities. The belief that youths can be isolated from their groups and that their behaviors can be altered as if group and community influences don't exist is, from our experience, unrealistic and a waste of resources. AFY's approach to working with the gang as a very cohesive neighborhood friendship group is congruent with the views of Dawley (1992) and Morales (1992) who concluded that neighborhood adolescent gangs are essentially friendship groups whose members are not inordinately disturbed and who exhibit positive characteristics that can be exploited to redirect behaviors into constructive channels. These groups, we have found, are often responsive to outreach offers of service.

The fundamental hypothesis upon which RT rests is, "Destructive behaviors can be redirected into constructive behaviors when youths believe that they matter." The practice of RT is directed at helping youths believe that they have worth and value, that they have competencies to become successful in conventional society, that their efforts to succeed will have a gratifying payoff, and that they do matter.

Since gang members are, for the most part, low-income minorities, a view subscribed to by most researchers (Thrasher, 1928, Spergel, 1992), it is easy for the mainstream to be indifferent to them and simply not care about the conditions that generated their gangs in the first place, or for that matter to even care about them as human beings. They are, to mainstream society, just faceless kids from the bad part of town. It has been said that indifference kills, and in the case of poor minority kids it is too often literally true. Physical death may only be the last stage of a process in which hope and spirit have already died, leaving in its place anger and despair. Destructive rampages bring out calls to break up the gangs, but in the long term what Morales called the Law Enforcement Institutional or "break them up" approach appears doomed to fail, because as long as gang members live in the same neighborhood and find a compelling need to affiliate, they will affiliate (Shaw, 1971, p. 100). The hypothesis that the fear of outside threats increases cohesion (Cartwright and Zander, 1968) certainly applies to the gang, which often sees the police as just another powerful gang (Catterall, July 5, 1991). The prevailing law-enforcement approach to the youth gang problem appears to have had the opposite effect from the one intended. Instead of breaking them up, they tend to become more cohesive and stronger. Threats, street justice, and arrests, which only deepen anger and alienation, may have a short-term salutary effect, but in the end, the gangs appear to prevail.

AFY began to practice a version of Carl Rogers's Person-Centered Therapy as early as 1989, and found that the adjustments dictated by its client population, which was markedly different from Rogers's affluent, mostly Caucasian, clients, had really evolved into a new pediatric methodology tailored to a young low-income minority population. From 1989 through 2009, AFY worked with over thirty-five gangs. Additionally, much work has been conducted with groups from several schools, mostly high schools, that bear characteristics very similar to gangs. Gangs have ranged in size from under ten members to over one hundred. The larger gangs are usually composed of several factions. One of the very large groups has periodically conducted sophisticated reunions that may be attended by over two hundred people, including wives and girlfriends. The group has not been identified as a gang for many years, but its members still retain their friendships to a greater or lesser degree. The group includes college graduates, entrepreneurs, and musicians, and even a social worker with an MSW degree who is on the AFY staff.

Before we wrote our 1996 book, we were disheartened to learn, from a review of the literature, that gang intervention programs, historically, had a very weak record. Miller (1990, p. 267) after examining sixty gang programs from 1920–1985, found that they had been generally ineffective, and Spergel (1992, p. 136) observed that nothing in the literature, "suggests clearly how to effectively address youth gang problems." On the other hand, it appeared that some promising programs never had a chance to prove themselves, due to political meddling and subsequent loss of funding. One such program was the Boston Midcity Project that ran from 1954–1957. It included outreach staff and broad community participation. It appeared to be moving in the right direction but was terminated at the end of its three-year demonstration period (Miller, 1959). AFY averted this fate by learning how to raise its own money, and becoming a private, non-profit corporation. A large-scale community organization effort in the early 1960s, Mobilization For Youth, also failed.

Cloward and Ohlin (1960), the authors of *Delinquency and Opportunity Theory*, which later emerged as Mobilization for Youth (MFY), a $10 million-a-year, three-year project strongly supported by President John F. Kennedy and funded by Congress, believed, since delinquency and gangs were products of the social system and not of individuals, community restructuring was the answer to the problem. They and Yablonsky (1962) believed, based on historic failures, that extending services to delinquent individuals and violent gang members was futile. Subsequently, the New York-based MFY became the "blueprint" for communities throughout the nation. It came to a screeching halt in 1964, after five years of planning and two years of implementation. New York City officials charged that the organization was "riot-producing, communist-oriented, left-wing, and corrupt," (Weissman, 1969). Despite MFY's failure, Delinquency and Opportunity Theory persists as a powerful influence in human-service thought.

MFY appears to have failed for two important reasons. The first, despite Grosser's belief that "consumers of social welfare services can define their problems and goals and negotiate on their own turf," (Grosser, in Brager and Purcell, 1967), is the reality that there is no single consumer. There are multiple consumers and multiple organizations competing to represent them. Conversely, there are forces representing the status quo, standing in opposition to any grass-roots effort that will upset the apple cart. The opposition to change, e.g., local government and businesses, often has more money and is better organized. Grass-roots organizations all too often end up competing among themselves. The second is the failure to recognize that no single population, especially a population as volatile and alienated as youth gangs, can be ignored without serious consequences. AFY strongly believes that successful programs begin from the bottom up, with individuals and small groups, and not from the top down, through edicts. Cornerstone principles of Redirectional Therapy are self-determination and the acceptance of responsibility for one's decisions.

The problem back then was an absence of knowledge on how to help change behaviors of these youths. The popularity of Cloward and Ohlin's decision to ignore them may simply have been an expression of frustration from not having a therapeutic alternative. Unfortunately, this limited view has persisted. In 1994 an *Arkansas Democrat-Gazette* reporter, while doing an interview with AFY, quoted an unnamed, "national authority" on youth issues who said, "In my opinion we should just write off this generation of youths." Hers was a position no different, perhaps, than banishing lepers, before drug treatments were discovered in the 1940s. When you don't know what to do, the common practice seems to be to let the afflicted stew in their own juices. AFY decided to look for answers, and believes it is on the right track.

The practice of RT has demonstrated that it is an effective means for redirecting youths from destructive gang behaviors to constructive social organization behavior. These young people have shown that they have the ability to merge successfully with the social and economic mainstream.

Highly skilled clinicians are uncommon in youth services, and especially in the youth gang field. Much more familiar to gang work are "rehabilitated" gang members. In fact Hagedorn (1988) and Spergel (1992) were strong advocates "for training and hiring former gang members," no doubt because mental health professionals didn't want to and didn't know how to do the work. Perhaps this speaks to the failure of gang-intervention programs, and even more importantly confirms the view that since work with this population is "futile" anyway, why spend real money on it when the illusion of doing something is enough. Other issues related to staffing gang programs are the fears engendered by working with gangs and working in gang and high-crime communities, and the fear many professionals have of simply working with groups. Office visits are encounters that take place on the therapist's turf. The gang worker, on the other hand, is working in what is perceived as a dangerous environment on the client's turf.

Any group can generate more power than an individual, and a gang is perceived as being especially powerful, and, therefore, very scary. The clinician working on the street leaves all the traditional counseling props behind. All she/he has are her/his skills and knowledge. Is it any wonder that gang work is not often the career choice of mental health professionals, thus leaving the task of working with youth gangs to anyone willing to do it?

A very special kind of professional is the one who has experienced the gang life and has gone on to earn a degree. There is little that can substitute for life experience combined with professional knowledge and skill, but still there is no guarantee that even this person can be an effective gang clinician. Temperament is so critical.

AFY clinicians, as a rule, work with a minimum of four groups. Often they are engaged with a mix of gang and school therapy groups.

While approaches, mostly through charismatic gang workers, to alter youth gangs and violence may have been successful, there has been no replicable therapeutic approach, of which we are aware, prior to RT. This therapy presents a teachable, clearly identifiable, and replicable change model that has, heretofore, never been part of the violent youth and gang change equation.

AFY proposes that the practice of RT can make a significant difference in reducing youth violence and gangs on the street. We see it as a cost-effective new "medicine" to resolve a persistent problem that makes both human and economic sense.

This book has been written for everyone with a brain and a heart. If we advance a belief that gangs and alienated youths are worthy of, and responsive to help, and that youths, by improving their lives, are creating a safer, healthier, and more stable environment for everyone, our effort will have served a good purpose.

Chapter 2

A Group Theory Perspective of Gangs

A youth gang is, first and foremost, a group, and, as such, each has its own syntality (group personality). Groups are infinitely more complex than individuals, given that not only is the clinician working with the uniqueness of each group but also the unique personalities of its members. Despite the inherent differences among gangs it appears that they share fundamental commonalities. They are either a small friendship group, with a core membership rarely exceeding twenty-five members, or a larger group, divided into factions. Members frequently live in the same neighborhood and share common age, economic, ethnic, gender, experiential, and interest characteristics.

Many if not most gang members believe that they do not fit into, nor are they acceptable to, the mainstream. Not now and not ever. They feel in many ways that their ethnicity and poverty makes them different, and because of their color that they, literally, wear their fate on their faces. Their low self-esteem is reinforced by history. They have experienced few educated or occupationally successful role models, and violence, including domestic violence, appears to be a fact of life.

Consequently, they believe they have little worth, and since they are unloved, that they are unlovable. They also feel powerless to change their lives, and often, even if they do want to change, don't know how to go about doing it.

Many gang members have traveled very little outside of their own neighborhood and have had little contact with people different from themselves. The gang is the brotherhood, sometimes sisterhood, that provides security, a sense of belonging, affection, and value. Because these youths have so little, what they do have becomes exaggerated in importance. They protect their small turf, called the neighborhood, stake out their territory when they go to school, fight to establish dominance, steal because it provides instant gratification and generates excitement, and become truant because they don't anticipate any payoff from attending school.

Middle-class youths are often willing to postpone gratification because they believe they can improve their position in life. Gang youths, on the other hand, don't believe they have a future, and, therefore, live mostly in the here-and-now. Youths have told AFY that they saw no point in attending school because they didn't expect to live long enough to graduate anyway.

The poverty and ethnicity of gang members set them apart from the social mainstream, which, consequently, has little empathy for them and deems them unworthy of concern. The attitude that they exist beyond the boundaries of "decent" society and are threatening objects to be feared, hated, and destroyed is not lost on gang members. The police may only add to the stereotype by its own creation of the "gang profile," which subjects youths, whose appearances deviate from the mainstream, to harassment. In turn, gang members, who already feel vulnerable, cloak themselves, often literally, in their tough guy images for protection against other gangs.

"Cohesiveness" refers to the spirit of the group, the "we" feeling that joins people together to form a single unit. "On an individual level, cohesiveness refers to each member's attraction to other group members," including how much s/he likes, respects, and trusts them. "Furthermore, because those who are members of cohesive groups tend to remain in the group for a longer period of time," scholarly definitions of cohesiveness often focus on membership maintenance (Forsyth, 1983, p. 349). Cartwright (1968, p. 91) defined cohesiveness as "the degree to which the members of the group desire to remain in their group," and Festinger (1950, p. 274) called it "the resultant of all the forces acting on the member to remain in the group." For the gang the "we" feeling is strengthened by its symbols, including group name, hand signs, clothing, including colored "rags," and control of its "turf." In this respect the gang is not unlike many other groups including fraternities, police, scouts, the military, and religious organizations.

Often gang traditions are passed on from generation to generation. Thus, some gangs, as suggested by their intergenerational nature, are among the most highly cohesive groups in society. "In closely knit groups, members tend to participate more fully and communicate more frequently while absences are much less likely," (Forsyth, 1983, p. 352). Furthermore, people in cohesive groups experience heightened self-esteem and lowered anxiety because the group provides a perceived source of identity, security, and protection. Such groups also have been found to be more effective than groups with low cohesion in achieving goals that the members themselves consider to be important. As cohesion increases, the group's capacity to retain its members also tends to increase. Thus, cohesiveness "contributes to a group's potency and vitality; it increases the significance of membership for those who belong to the group," (Cartwright and Zander, 1968, p. 91).

The gang provides a sense of togetherness and protection. Gang members appear to be youths who feel less in control of their lives than others within a low-income minority community that already sees itself as powerless. It appears axiomatic that the less power one feels, the lower is one's self-esteem. Among gang members, low self-esteem appears to be a common characteristic. They don't believe they have the capacity for success in the mainstream, and therefore affiliate with other "losers" like themselves. The gang appears to provide an increased sense of power and control, and therefore gang membership appears to improve self-esteem. Turf is protected because it provides a sense of ownership and power.

The view that all gangs form with the intent to do harm appears to be a myth. In fact, Adult Friends for Youth has found that many gang members regret that they and their friends have to be a gang, and they wish things were different. Few have said they joined the gang to cause trouble or joined with the intent to harm. Most have stated that the gang provides protection; "Your brothers protect your back and you protect their backs." However, this doesn't cancel the attitude that "sometimes the best defense is a strong offense." It is not uncommon to believe that by acting aggressively you may reduce threats that may be made against you.

"The negative aspect of highly cohesive groups is that they exert a more powerful influence over their members than do groups with low cohesion," (Forsyth, 1983, p. 353). Festinger (1950) found that when an individual is not strongly attracted to the group and is being pressured to perform undesirable behaviors, s/he will resist the behavior or simply terminate membership. In highly cohesive groups, however, the pressure to remain in the group is very powerful. It appears to be self-imposed, as well as imposed by other members. Therefore, the gang has a correspondingly high degree of influence over its members.

When gangs feel threatened by outside forces, they, not unlike military units, establish their own rules of behavior, because in that time and place the group may be the only reality that exists for them. The norms and laws of the greater social system are consequently diminished. The greater the sense of threat, the greater is the "we-they" feeling. Social exchange theory suggests that cohesive groups offer members a satisfying high reward/cost ratio, and that this is especially true for core members who have the greatest stake in the group (Thibaut and Kelley, 1959).

While the ability of cohesive groups to "exert a more powerful influence over their members," has potentially negative consequences, the opposite also appears to be true (Forsyth, 1983, p. 353). For example, it has often been found that older, highly influential youths can contribute to the positive change of younger members. In other words, as older members begin to develop more prosocial attitudes and behaviors, they may become positive role models for younger members. Peer pressure that previously resulted in destructive behavior may subsequently result in pressure to conform to socially acceptable behavior. A ripple effect is thus established. Further, it has been observed that as one gang moves toward prosocial behavior it has the potential to influence other gangs.

At Kalihi's Farrington High School Commencement in 1992, at which five members of the notorious Junior Sons of Samoa graduated (a first), a conversation among members of a rival group was overheard in which one member said, "If they can do it, so can we." The comment suggested the possibility that a new standard of competition could be established. In fact, over time, graduation rates for the Juniors, as well as for other groups, have increased significantly. Almost all members of the Baby Hawaii Brothers and the Sons of Samoa hierarchy, which included the Juniors, Peewees, and Baby Gangsters, have graduated. Rates prior to 1992 were approximately 20 percent.

A survey of students conducted in March 1995 revealed that for academic years 1993 and 1994, high school graduation rates increased significantly, from 20 to 70 percent. Among the seventy-nine students who had reached age eighteen, fifty-five had graduated, and twenty-four had either dropped out or had been forced out. Comparisons between gang members from the predominant ethnic groups that AFY serves revealed that twenty-seven Samoan students or members of a Samoan group (N=30), 90 percent, had graduated; and twenty-eight Filipino students or members of a Filipino group (N=49), 57 percent, had graduated. It should be noted that non-Samoans and non-Filipinos may also be members of these groups.

An additional insight was provided by exploring what happened to the survey group of seventy-nine students after completing high school. We found that 87 percent of the seventy-five students about whom information was available were either working full-time or were pursuing higher education. Eight, 10 percent, had been arrested.

Members of groups with whom we have worked are moving in a mainstream direction, and the movement appears to be contagious.

Only a few years earlier, most of these youths expressed the belief that prison was inevitable and the chance of survival to old age was remote. Prior to the beginning of AFY's service, hopelessness, especially expressed by Samoan youths, almost certainly led them to unemployment and prison. A dramatic shift occurred. The inevitability of incarceration became remote, and living to a ripe old age became a common expectation. In their own words, they were "mellowing out."

Undeniably, the gang has a powerful influence over its members. It promotes bonding and strong friendships, and consequently, efforts to break it up and to get kids out of it are almost always doomed to failure. Therefore, if behaviors are to be changed, the group cannot be ignored, as it is both the context and means of that change. Just as the group will be the context in which change will occur, Adult Friends for Youth has developed Redirectional Therapy as the means for facilitating the group's change.

Redirectional Therapy emerged from an appreciation of certain basic realities about intervention with youth gangs:

1. It takes place on their turf.
2. AFY has no legal authority or power over them.
3. Direct pressure from other systems, including the school, police, courts, parents, and other programs, has not been successful.

Therefore, an alternative that was nondirective and accepted gang members, with all their warts, seemed to make sense. The closest approach at hand was Carl Rogers's Person-Centered Therapy.

AFY's approach to working with youth gangs, while resting on a Person-Centered philosophical foundation, evolved into a new and distinct therapy with values and principles of its own. The evolution is natural enough, given the uniqueness of the target population. RT is an ever-evolving therapy that now has a history of two decades.

Chapter 3

Redirectional Therapy Philosophy

Redirectional Therapy (RT) stands on two legs, philosophy and practice. Philosophy is the body of principles that guide practice. It provides the framework within which practice is conducted, and defines the way in which Adult Friends for Youth views people, and, specifically, how it views its clients. Practice is doing what we preach and will be presented in Chapter IV.

Much of RT's philosophy is owed to humanistic psychology, existential thought, and the Person-Centered Method of Carl Rogers, approaches that present the perspective that each person is a product of his or her own set of experiences, and, therefore, has a unique internal frame of reference. The basic tenet of this "third force" of psychotherapy (the other two being Freudianism and behaviorism) is that people are free to choose, but must accept the consequences of their decisions within the limits of prevailing values, social customs, and laws.

Existentialism takes the view that life is not predetermined and inevitable, but that we are active players in molding what we are and what we become, and that to become the person we want to be takes ceaseless effort (Belkin, 1987). The burden of decision-making within this process is on the individual, and not on any other party, including professional helpers.

Rogers, early in his career, began to see the validity of a therapist who was nondirective and did not give suggestions or advice. He emphasized the importance of relationships and believed that within a warm, trusting environment the client can make his or her own constructive decisions (Corey, 1990, pp. 284-285). In his view, growth and change were most likely to occur when the therapist exhibited a warm, positive, and accepting attitude toward the client. He saw this relationship as a "kind of love" in which the person feels "prized" or valued in a complete way and not for a particular behavior of the moment.

He held in high regard the concept of not making judgments and took the position that "prizing" the client is independent of the client's behavior. To illustrate his point he offered a quote from a colleague:

> I am beginning to feel that the key to the human being is the attitudes with which the parents have regarded him. If the child was lucky enough to have parents who have felt proud of him, wanted him just as he was, exactly as he was, this child grows into adulthood with self-confidence, self-esteem; he goes forth in life feeling sure of himself, strong, able to lick what confronts him. Franklin Delano Roosevelt is an example. He couldn't imagine anyone thinking otherwise. He had two adoring parents. He was like the pampered dog that runs up at you, frisking his tail, eager to love you, for this dog has never known rejection or harshness. Even if you should kick him, he'll come right back to you, his tail friskier than ever, thinking you're playing a game with him and wanting more. This animal cannot imagine anyone disapproving or disliking him. Just as unconditional regard and love was poured into him, he has it now to give out. If a child is lucky enough to grow up in this unconditionally accepting atmosphere, he emerges as strong and sure, and he can approach life and its vicissitudes with courage and confidence, with zest and joy of expectation.

> "But the parents who like their children — if. They would like them if they were changed, altered, different; if they were smarter or if they were better, or if, if, if. The offspring of these parents have trouble because they never had the feeling of acceptance. These parents don't really like these children; they would like them if they were like someone else. When you come down to the basic fundamental, the parents feel; "I don't like this child, this child before me." They don't say that. I am beginning to believe that it would be better for all concerned if parents did. It wouldn't leave such horrible ravages on these unaccepted children. It's never done that crudely. 'If you were a nice boy and did this, that, and the other thing, then we would all love you.'
>
> "I am coming to believe that children brought up by parents who would like them "if" are never quite right. They grow up assuming that their parents are right and that they are wrong; that somehow or other they are at fault; and even worse, very frequently they feel they are stupid, inadequate, inferior (Rogers, 1962)."

Rogers concluded that there is an extraordinary contrast between an unconditional positive regard and a conditional regard. He believed, further, that the message was just as powerful for counselors as for parents.

A comparison between the idealized upbringing of a child for whom the sky is the limit and the impoverished minority youths with whom we work explains why one may become president and the other joins a gang. Many of our kids can't imagine any adult liking them unconditionally. They feel prejudged, because of their race or ethnicity, their poverty, the social standing of their parents, where they live, and even the reputation of the school they attend. Parents worn down by life often send the message that "This child is just another burden to me." Under this heavy weight of parental and social rejection, how can the child feel anything but stupid, frustrated, worthless, and inferior? And how can s/he be expected to become anything other than angry and violent?

The Rogerian method has been supported by three tenets. In addition to unconditional positive regard, it has rested on authenticity, or genuineness, and empathy. Genuineness is the ability of the therapist to express his or her own feelings about the client's behavior and utterances by giving "I" messages. The authentic therapist is able to say, "I worry about what will happen to you when you fight." This is different from presuming to tell someone else how to behave as suggested by the order, "You shouldn't fight." The Person-Centered therapist doesn't use shoulds or shouldn'ts, and is not an authority figure. In one of our alternative education classes a student continued to talk to another student during a lesson. The clinician/teacher, AFY's current President and CEO, Deborah L.K. Spencer-Chun, addressed him by saying, "Chris, I feel disrespected when you keep talking during the lesson. Have I ever disrespected you?" Chris sheepishly acknowledged that Deb had only treated him with respect and that he owed her that. This exchange could only have worked where a trusting mutual relationship already existed.

Empathy is the ability to sense the other person's inner world of meanings as if they were your own, "but without ever losing the 'as if' quality." Having this sense allows the helper to move about freely in the client's world and to express meanings and feelings about which the clients may be only vaguely aware. The ability to listen and feel acutely so that the client knows that s/he is understood is not easy to achieve, but, when it happens, it may provide the potential for the greatest change to occur.

Rogers understood the rarity of this level of understanding. He said that we usually only go so far as to say, "I understand what is wrong with you," or, "I understand what makes you act that way." These are value judgments. True understanding is difficult to achieve because it makes us uncomfortable. Rogers believed that we fear being open to the way other people experience life for fear of being changed ourselves, and change is something we all tend to resist. The result is that we view the world of others on our terms, which leads us to analyze and evaluate them (Rogers, 1962). Commonly, we respond to the act and ignore the humanity behind it. Empathy requires understanding the experiences and thoughts that precede behavior.

Equipped with this understanding it will be possible to better understand the theory and principles of RT. It is important to recognize, however, the difference between owing a debt of gratitude to what has come before and being only a shadow of it. Where, historically, psychiatry and psychology have strongly influenced the development of social work practice (Sarri, 1992, p. 41), RT is a unique methodology that has emerged from practice with low-income minority clients. It is a new way to approach gang youths and can be applied whether one is a student of other psychotherapies or not.

The Rogerian Person-Centered approach has been applied with mostly self-actualizing, articulate, and fairly well-to-do adult participants who are, primarily, interested in enhancing their capacity for personal growth. The population for RT is different in almost every respect. Nevertheless, despite differences in the target populations of these two methods, common values include a belief in the capacity for change and growth in all human beings, a belief that people are motivated to change once they believe in their capacity to do so, and a belief that self-determination leads to personal responsibility.

RT's initial goal is to ignite the fire that illuminates what is possible. The ultimate goal is to integrate gang members and other "violent" youths into the social and economic mainstream. Experience has demonstrated that behavioral controls and law-abiding behavior occur naturally as acculturation takes place and youths evolve from subcultural delinquent behavior into the mainstream.

It has been observed that as gang members begin to experience tangible rewards within the system, e.g., adult approval, improved school grades, approval from successful peers, participation and recognition in organized activities, graduation, jobs, and higher education, they begin to see themselves as "haves" rather than "have-nots." When this occurs, they appear to be less likely to commit acts that will jeopardize their achievements.

A significant event that underlines this conclusion occurred in 1995. Two members of a public housing group with whom we had a long-standing relationship were killed, within days of each other, in separate incidents, by members of a group residing in another project. After the first killing, outside of a bar, some boys took it on themselves to go after the other group on its turf. A second young man died as a result. The situation cried out for retaliation, not only to avenge the deaths, but also to uphold the reputation of the housing project. In the past, reputation alone would have been enough to get a war on. In fact the OGs, men in their twenties and thirties were goading the younger boys to uphold the honor of "our place." Expectations, based on history, led everyone to expect retaliation to be imminent.

The project where the offending gang resided was secured by housing security and the police. Tensions were boiling over. Community leaders, including the clergy, did their best to calm things down. However, in the end it was AFY staff members who resolved the problem successfully. The group, many of whose members had already started to move on with their lives, had begun to surrender their gang-banging mentality. They were helped by staff to explore the consequences of retaliation, and comprehended that even if they prevailed, the cost in destruction, subsequent incarceration, and even death would be devastating.

At an earlier time, none of this would have mattered, since they believed that they had so little to live for anyway; only the group and turf meant anything. It defined who they were. But, times had changed. The group's cohesion had declined significantly. Members had developed individual identities and goals that were very distinct from the group. School and work were going well and they had developed a vision of a better life for themselves. As a body they were no longer willing to sacrifice their personal achievements for the group, and since nearly all of them had moved on there was little pressure to conform to historic beliefs. When they began to absorb the consequences of retaliation they concluded, collectively, that it was a bad idea. The staff effort that had gotten them to that point was no small thing, but it was possible only because of the years of work that had gone before.

Alinsky (1972) hypothesized that the "have-nots" are dangerous because they have no hope and, therefore, nothing to lose. The "haves" are smug and complacent. The "have a little-want mores" are the most productive, because they are aware of the potential that lies ahead and strive to achieve it. The latter position pretty much sums up the place in the road to which the boys had traveled.

The foundation of RT lies in the belief that the gang life, but not the group itself, is unacceptable even to most gang members. The reason for this is that no rational person wants to wake up each morning wondering if they will survive the day, and certainly, as Morales (1992) pointed out, most gang members are rational.

RT presumes that gang members, in most instances, have the ability to make decisions that are in their best interests, and, also, it presumes that they have the capacity to join the mainstream. Frequent opportunities for participating in new experiences are, therefore, provided by practitioners of the method. Examples are visits to institutions of higher education, participating in activities outside of the neighborhood, and eating at sit-down restaurants in middle-class neighborhoods.

Many of these youths have no idea that they can go to college, because all too often they've heard that they are "not college material." The mere action of taking them to a university removes the mystique and provides them with the sense that maybe it's possible after all. Eating in a restaurant where choices are required concerning the salad dressing and which fork to use, and where people look, talk, and dress differently, can be pretty scary at first, but when you survive and have fun you don't feel so different after all. New experiences can provide access to the "other world."

RT takes the position that gang members, while experiencing all the normal adjustments required of adolescents, also suffer from specific deficits (handicaps), not unlike those experienced by others who are disabled, and that with appropriate intervention they can overcome those deficits. Among these deficits is the experience of living in a brutal social environment and in families who often exhibit the following characteristics and circumstances:

1. Historic poverty
2. Minority ethnic and/or racial status
3. No, or limited, traditions of learning and scholarship
4. Few, or no, educated role models
5. Crowded living conditions that provide little, if any, privacy
6. Second-class status, through several generations, with the consequence that the condition has become endemic
7. Few, if any, social, educational or economic successes

These circumstances often make it difficult to face the day. Imagine the fear of walking out the front door not knowing whether you are going to survive to walk back through that door. Life under these conditions becomes a series of traumas, so is it any wonder that alcohol and drug use are common? Unless young people have hope for a life relatively free of fear, pain, and economic instability, the other problems that we use as high-risk identifiers, such as education failure, delinquency, crime, drug and alcohol abuse, violence, self-destruction, incarceration, mental and physical illness, homelessness, premature and bad parenting, joblessness, perpetual poverty, abuse of others, and premature death are not going to be resolved. The trauma of poverty cannot be swept under the rug. It is a major issue in solving the problem of gangs.

A fundamental belief of AFY and RT is that "destructive behaviors can be redirected into constructive behaviors when youths believe that they matter." Helping youths believe that they matter is a major plateau to be reached on the road to change. Therefore, the Redirectionalist, unlike the behaviorist, does not dwell on specific behaviors, e.g., fighting, school failure, drug use, nor on the severity of these behaviors, but rather focuses on the person's abilities and his/her value as a human being. Regardless of the individual's problems and behaviors, s/he is presumed to be fundamentally okay with the potential to become a constructive, contributing person within the social and economic mainstream.

Building on these fundamentals are the philosophical principles of RT that follow:

1. **People have the capacity to change.** Behaviors are not immutable, but are subject to all the influences of the environment, both physical and emotional. RM accepts the existential view that life is not predetermined and inevitable, but that we are active players in molding who we are and what we become. The Redirectionalist, as a significant person to the client and group, influences change. Consequently, even though change may be slow in coming, the Redirectionalist persistently pursues it. Therefore, it may be necessary to provide service over several years. Commonly, groups receive three to four years of service, and some individuals many years more.
2. **People are perceived holistically as products of the sum total of their existence.** Therefore, as experiences are altered, attitudes and behaviors also change. Clients are not defined by their problems, e.g., drug abuse, violence, or crime, nor are they approached with a therapy to fix a specific problem. Destructive behaviors are viewed as a response to life experiences that can be altered as an outcome of new life experiences. However, attitudes and behaviors are conditioned over time, and over time beliefs are established that condition the way we respond to stimuli, e.g., if you believe that people are violent and brutal by nature then the only way to survive is to become more violent and brutal than the next guy.

   In our experience it is almost impossible to isolate one social problem from others. An attempt to work on an issue such as substance abuse without taking into account the back story and other related issues is, in our view, self-defeating in the long term. This isn't to say that where there are physiological addictions that

AFY doesn't make appropriate referrals, but such a referral would be just one measure in a total treatment program.

We also do not apply psychiatric diagnostic labels to clients. We do not want them to view themselves as "sick," or to use a label as an excuse for destructive behaviors, e.g., "I can't help myself because I have a behavior disorder." By practicing holistically we avoid compartmentalizing people. Instead, we take the view that we are all multifaceted, with strengths that lead to satisfying and productive lives and weaknesses that torment us and others.

The use of labels would also pose a dilemma for the Redirectionalist, who claims to be nonjudgmental. To avoid having youths judged when they are out in public, AFY goes so far as having no identifying logo or name on agency vehicles.

Existentially, people are free to choose, but they are responsible for their choices. Gang members have needs and emotions common to all human beings, and will, we believe, as their physical and emotional needs are met, become increasingly at peace with themselves and the world around them.

3. **Gang youths have the potential to enter the social and economic mainstream but may not believe that they have the capacity to do so.** The Redirectionalist freely and frequently emphasizes competencies that enhance the youth's perception that s/he is a capable person who can choose to enter the mainstream. The mainstream is defined as a position in life that, minimally, includes several, but not necessarily all, of the following achievements:

    a. A high school diploma or the equivalent.
    b. Employment in a permanent job that provides opportunities for advancement.
    c. Attendance in or completion of a higher education program (includes vocational programs.)
    d. Good feelings about one's self-worth.
    e. Obeying the law.

f. Avoiding physical confrontations.
g. Engaging in normative social behaviors, e.g., abstaining from swearing, roughhousing, shouting, or spitting in public areas.
h. Participating in social clubs and engaging in public service.

4. **Youths who believe in their capacity to enter the mainstream will choose to do so when provided with the opportunity.** When low-income, minority children are asked what they want to be when they grow up, their responses are not unlike those of their middle-class peers. The difference appears later in the execution of their plans. Often they lack both the self-confidence and knowledge to pursue their dreams. However, when someone else whom they care about, demonstrates belief in and support for their goals and helps them understand how they can get there, they also begin to believe in them. Frequently, they begin to strive toward achieving what, at an earlier time, may have only been a fantasy.
5. **Most people have the capacity to make decisions that are in their best interests, but may require support, encouragement, and information before they believe they are capable of doing so.** It is difficult, if not impossible for anyone, much less adolescents, to believe that they have the ability to make decisions that are good for them when almost every experience that they have tells them that they can't. Most gang kids grow up in families and neighborhoods where many things that happen are bad. All around them they experience joblessness, substandard housing, crowding, violence, noise, dependency on government and/or charity, crime, drugs, and poverty. There is not much that instills feelings of worth and self-confidence. Mostly their feelings are of the other sort—that they are losers among losers. Too often they hear that they will never amount to anything. Why wouldn't they live down to the expectations that others have of them?

   As a second-year social work student, Sid remembers being raked over the coals by his practicum instructor for having the audacity to take his gang on a trip to a university campus. He was told that he was giving them an unrealistic idea of what they could become. He didn't believe then, nor obviously has he changed his mind since, that people have to be limited by their histories. Upon graduating from AFY's alternative school, a student expressed in his commencement address that the difference between AFY and his high school, and even his family, was that people were always telling him "you can't," when AFY was telling him "you can."

The practicum instructor was wrong. Four years after obtaining his MSW degree, Sid became the director of Sophie Wright Settlement in Detroit. "The Players" was a gang with whom the agency worked. One member, Derek Brown, subsequently went on to earn his MSW and eventually became the settlement's executive director. As was noted earlier, AFY more recently had a similar experience when Malakai Maumalanga earned his MSW. He is currently the agency's clinical coordinator.

It takes time and skill to establish a group culture within which members develop the comfort to be open and share their deepest emotions, try out their thoughts and plans, and gain the confidence to act on them. Over time, as successful decisions are made and rewards are forthcoming, the capacity to make good decisions increases as part of a natural developmental progression.

6. **A mutual and respectful relationship between the Redirectionalist and the client is a prelude to effective intervention.** Unlike other psychotherapies, the Redirectionalist more often than not works on the client's turf. AFY does not accept mandated referrals from law enforcement, judiciary, educational, child welfare, or any other system. Non-mandated referrals are accepted and encouraged as long as there is no actual or implied consequence if service is refused. AFY tries hard to make its services attractive, and nearly always succeeds, but the final decision to accept or reject it is always made, without prejudice of any sort, by the potential client. Service cannot proceed unless the individual

and the group know that the decision to enter into a relationship is their decision alone, and that they can terminate it at their discretion. A relationship that does not foster mutuality and self-determination from the beginning would make a mockery of AFY's nondirective and nonjudgmental approach to treatment.

Both the gang and AFY engage in the relationship with each other freely, as equals, based on a belief that each can use it to satisfy its needs. This belief appears to be common to all relationships engaged in freely. At the beginning of the relationship a feeling-out process takes place, as the partners explore each other's needs and interests. Goals, at first, will no doubt be cloudy, and each may have agendas that are not revealed to the other. A former gang member noted in a newspaper interview (Sunday *Star-Bulletin and Advertiser*, Feb. 14, 1993), "At first we thought, yeah—this Adult Friends for Youth is going to take us all over the place so we can have fun. It was fun, but we also found out that they can help us with our problems." His group's agenda clearly was to take advantage of an opportunity to have the agency spend money on them and to manipulate it without any expectation that the experience would change them. Ultimately, our goals coincided. Police officers have expressed the opinion, "You really don't understand them. They're just using you." This attitude has also translated into the conclusion that AFY is promoting gangs, i.e., if they are using us we must be encouraging them.

In a better world, law enforcement would understand that its short-term goal of protecting the community in the here and now and AFY's long-term goal of making the community safe in the future are compatible. In other words, an understanding and respectful relationship that would allow law enforcement to do what it needs to do to protect lives and property in the moment, and allow AFY to do what it can do to improve lives and make change permanent for a better tomorrow, would be the ideal relationship. From time to time we have arrived at that place.

Our long-term goal is to improve lives and create hope for a better life, free from violence, crime, gangs, and drugs. When we enter into a relationship we begin with what we identify as the "seductive phase" of the relationship.

In this initial seductive phase, the Redirectionalist provides fun, e.g., movies, the beach, sports, and an abundance of food as a means for establishing an environment where youths would rather be with AFY than be anywhere else. Members of the group also experience psychic rewards that include having someone who listens, accepts them as they are in a give-and-take relationship, communicates respect, doesn't judge them by their behavior, doesn't talk down to them, and sees them as a friend. A bonus for receiving service is contact with other staff members who also relate to them in a respectful and dignified manner.

Activities and food are not provided as a reward for good behavior. They are provided because they are believed to have intrinsic therapeutic value.

We have been occasionally challenged by educators and others who wonder about "bad" kids being provided with pleasurable experiences. Pleasure reinforces negative behavior is their view. In fact, the opposite appears to be true. Pleasure communicates unconditional positive regard. It is completely nonjudgmental and says, "I accept you as a person of worth just as you are. I may not like what you are doing, but no matter how you behave I still care about you."

Once youths believe that they are valued and begin to feel competent, the next step is to become self-determining and take responsibility for decision making and its outcomes.

The second phase, after the relationship and trust are established, begins when members feel free to openly discuss their lives and the difficulties that they are encountering, and begin to accept the Redirectionalist as an advocate, someone who really cares about them, understands their problems, and wants to help them. In this phase the Redirectionalist is also able to share his/her needs and to expect in return the respect he has shown for them. As an example, one group graffitied the agency van on a field trip, and was confronted on the basis of respect. The staff member asked, "Have I or AFY ever disrespected you?" The answer, of course was, "No." He followed up by expressing, genuinely, "I really felt disrespected when you graffitied the van. It makes me feel that you, also, don't respect AFY." This confrontation, like the one cited earlier with Deb, could only work because a mutually trusting and caring relationship had already been established. When the group became aware that someone who they cared about felt violated they apologized profusely and soon after cleaned up the van. The professional must be capable of drawing a line between an emotional response to destructive behavior and a controlled objective response. By being in control, the Redirectionalist is able to express a feeling about behavior without condemning the group or the person.

7. **The Redirectionalist and the agency provide an environment that is genuine, caring, and nurturing.** Expressions such as, "I care about you," "I believe in you," and "I love you guys," are therapeutically valued. AFY hypothesizes that love and/or being admired are the basic ingredients to achieving self-worth, and that they increase in value according to the importance of the source of the expression. The message being communicated is, "you are worth being valued because I value you," or in the words of Carl Rogers, "I prize you." For someone living in a desert devoid of affection, this is powerful stuff.

Many of the youths with whom we work, and, from our experience, gang youths in general, exist in a life position that Eric Berne (1964) identified as minus-minus (other life positions in Transactional Analysis being "plus-plus," [popularized as "I'm okay, you're okay"], "plus-minus," and "minus-plus"). He called the "minus-minus" position, or "I'm not okay, you're not okay," the most dangerous because it is simultaneously suicidal and homicidal. In other words, the youth believes that he is so worthless that he doesn't care if he lives or dies, or if anyone else lives or dies, either. Why, he believes, should I care about anyone, when no one cares about me? In its extreme, this is a very dangerous state of mind. An approach that includes threats or appeals to reason is surely doomed to fail. In order to have a chance at success this person must feel that s/he is cared about.

The long-term goal of RT is to change the life position from minus-minus to plus-plus through a nurturing group experience where group members feel genuinely valued and loved by each other, by the Redirectionalist, and by people whom they encounter, including teachers, peers, family, employers, and co-workers.

8. **The Redirectionalist is primarily responsible to the agency and to its clients, not to other systems, including school, police, courts, and parents.** Everyone who enters into a client relationship with AFY is a client of the agency, not of just the individual clinician. The clinician is an agent of AFY. There is, therefore, at the very least, an implied contract that requires the agency to represent the interests of its clients in relation to other institutions and parties. The Redirectionalist represents the agency and is expected to represent the adolescent's interests as an advocate, not unlike the role of advocate in the legal system. The agency must, while working cooperatively with other institutions, be independent of them. Failure to maintain this freedom is counterproductive, as it impairs trust, and thereby diminishes the potential for a long-term therapeutic relationship. A subservient relationship would include providing information on illegal activities to the police, failure to confront law enforcement when deemed necessary, agreeing with a parent who condemns a child as a "no good," and supporting a school that wants to deny service as a punishment. Various systems may be involved with our youths, including school, court, police, and family. However, they are not our clients and we don't represent them.

Additionally, since the probability is great that illegal activities are already taking place, there can be no point in attempting to establish a therapeutic relationship if the intent is to punish and control. There are already enough organizations doing that. An exception would be the legal requirement, established by *Tarasoff v. The Board of Regents of University of California*, (University of Pittsburgh Law Review, 1975), to notify the potential victim and law enforcement authorities when bodily harm to another person is threatened. The principle applied here, of course, is that the rights of the client leave off where the rights of others are endangered. Therefore, if the therapist has knowledge that a gang is threatening to injure another party, s/he is responsible for reporting it to the agency, and, if it appears that the agency cannot successfully intervene, to report it to the police.

Not long ago, conflicts between youths from two public housing communities flared into a severe beating, a stabbing, and a shooting in rapid succession. Both the police and AFY were aware of the lightning rod for these events. He had been targeted after a beating he had administered to a boy who showed up on his turf and threatened him. The severity of the beating put the boy in the hospital for several days. The stabbing and shooting were retaliations.

AFY and the police concurred that the heat could only be turned down if he left the area. The sticking point was that he was on probation, which prevented him from leaving the jurisdiction. Attempts by both the police and AFY to work with his probation officer failed. The commander of the police district agreed to contact the judge who had the case and ask her to temporarily lift the travel restriction, which she did. AFY paid for his fare to another island, where he lived for two weeks with a relative. Subsequently, a mediation at breakfast, between the two young men was conducted by AFY where the young man who suffered the beating acknowledged that he was so drunk when he went to the other's neighborhood that he didn't know what he was doing and had no recollection of going there or anything that took place afterwards. He only remembered waking up in ICU. During the mediation he accepted responsibility for his behavior. His attacker acknowledged he got caught up in the heat of the moment and became irrational. It wasn't until later that he became aware of the potential consequences to both his victim and himself. The young men spoke with each other, at length, during and following the formal mediation. They learned that they had much in common, including that they both had new baby daughters, born within two weeks of each other. They both agreed that their priorities now were taking care of their families, and not the "gang stuff."

9. **The client is always first.** The Redirectionalist's primary responsibility is to the agency and the agency's clients. Staff members, therefore, are committed to representing clients' best interests and advocating on their behalf. The reason that AFY exists is to help its clients become aware of their value and worth as human beings and the potential that they have to live stable, healthy, and constructive lives. We strive with our clients, both within the context of the group and in individual counseling, to develop an understanding of the people that they want to become and to help them in the process of achieving their goals.

   While an organization cannot survive without financing and accountability, it must always keep in mind that making more money and getting along with other institutions is not what it was established to do. When it finds itself spending more energy and effort to survive than it does on carrying out the purpose for which it was created in the first place, it should ask itself if it is still functional.

   At AFY, when a client enters the office, staff—and often its administrative staff—direct their attention to him/her. Sometimes it simply involves the exchange of pleasantries and a need to connect.

The aesthetics of the place where the agency does business sends a message. It should be attractive and well-maintained and give the impression that all who are part of the organization, especially staff members and clients, are valued. AFY's offices and meeting rooms are carpeted. Art, plaques, photos, and awards decorate the walls. Furniture is in keeping with a professional appearance.

The opposite also appears to be true. When a place is shabby and run down, it sends a message that this is a reflection of you and this is all you deserve.

The emotional quality, or "feel," of the agency, also has therapeutic value. It builds on the physical aesthetics of the office and by extension the appearance of agency vehicles. Collectively they communicate that being a participant in this organization is special and, therefore, I am special. We have found that barriers between groups have come down when they begin to see that they have the agency in common, and when they begin to identify themselves as an AFY group. Upon being threatened with the loss of AFY services by a law-and-order principal at Waipahu High School, several rival groups banded together and, in a collaborative effort, designed an AFY T-shirt that was worn by all on campus. This protest was triggered when the principal refused to consider their views on the importance of AFY's work with them. AFY continued to provide services throughout the principal's rocky tenure. She has since retired. When over one hundred youths attended on AFY "legislative assembly," they all wore a common AFY "Legislative Assembly" T-shirt. Staff members, by engaging in relationships with members of agency groups other than their own, promote both a feeling of oneness with the agency, and the sense that "you are also important to me." Inter-group activities also contribute to breaking down barriers.

Over the past several years, AFY has conducted a rugby tournament that has included youth teams from various Hawaii communities, Canada, New Zealand, and the United States mainland. It has provided an opportunity for its groups to play each other and to play other teams as well. The focus is on sportsmanship and making new friends through social activities, mostly involving food, that take place during the tournament. While the tournament is a fairly glitzy affair, AFY's groups arrange activities with each other throughout the year.

Total agency commitment is necessary if youths are really to feel that they come first. It has become clear that an effective gang-intervention program cannot be provided only on a redirectionalist-to-group, or redirectionalist-to-individual basis, and, perhaps, not even within a rigidly compartmentalized bureaucratic structure. Gang youths in crises can't be ignored if their staff member is unavailable. To communicate concern, the response must be immediate by anyone present, including other professional staff, clerical staff, and anyone else—if only to listen, but more if necessary, as long as it is within the staff member's level of competency.

All staff members, regardless of position, also become involved with large agency activities, such as the rugby tournament, the Student Transition Convention, involving ten thousand students across the state, and fund-raising. Agency groups and individual clients also help out. When staff and clients come together to support agency activities it enhances relationships. After a time, youths feel accepted and comfortable with all staff members, and feel, "I really belong here."

10. **Formal and informal education are means for achieving freedom, thinking critically, and becoming aware of a greater universe within which to make decisions.** While Redirectional Therapy is fundamentally non-value driven, there is one very important exception. Education is that exception. We believe strongly that education, whether academic or vocational, provides the freedom of choice. It is our belief that limited education chains low-income minority youths to limited opportunities within a range of narrow experiences.

Many of the young people with whom we work are first- or second-generation immigrants from the Philippines and Polynesia, who, when they enter the United States, take their place at the bottom of the social and economic ladder. The neighborhoods within which they settle are the ones that are often experiencing the highest rates of crime, drugs, violence, and gangs. In order to fit in and become accepted, they engage in the behaviors of their group. To the greater society these are deviant behaviors, but to the gang they may be normal. Soldiers may also accept deviant behavior as normative in a combat environment, because in that moment in time, all that matters is the group. This phenomenon that sociologists term "differential association" may partially explain how atrocities can be committed by otherwise law-abiding people.

Youths who are caught up in this lifestyle not infrequently feel there is no way out. They anticipate that their lives will be cut short or that they will end up in prison. Consequently, they question the value of school as well as their place outside of their neighborhoods. Thus, the inevitable occurs. With few options available, they become dangerous to themselves and others, and the self-fulfilling prophecy of prison and premature death or physical and mental disintegration becomes a reality. In a survey of its clients AFY found that over 30 percent were suicidal.

On the bright side, AFY has found that education can change this bleak scenario, and that students can be motivated to learn when helped and supported by their peers and by adults whom they trust. The Redirectionalist plays a key role in the process. AFY has also found that the regular school classroom may not work for many youths who fall into the high-risk category. For this reason it developed its own academic program which is conducted under the auspices of the Farrington High School Community School for Adults. The agency calls it the Clinical Competency-Based Alternative Education Program (C-Base).

What makes this program so different from other C-Base programs is that it is taught by clinical staff who can work with issues with which students are struggling while still carrying out the program's academic function. A recent class, consisting of twenty-three dropouts, had a 91 percent high school graduation rate. When one considers that in every case their high schools had given up on them and that in most instances they had also given up on themselves the outcome was quite remarkable. To eliminate bias, exams, monitoring, grading, and issuing of diplomas are conducted by Farrington adult education staff. Almost half of the 2007 class applied to a higher education program.

Since the beginning of AFY's gang program in 1989 the high school graduation rate for gang members has gone from less than 20 percent to over 70 percent.

11. **Children are capable of influencing their families.** The precept, "a child will lead them," has therapeutic value. It implies that as children change they initiate changes in their families and the world around them. As teachers and parents begin to see the child in a positive light, e.g., as a capable person, with admirable qualities, the child begins to see him/herself that way as well and performance improves accordingly. Parents and teachers, subsequently, feel better about themselves, and are more likely to work harder on behalf of the child.

    It has been observed that parents who have improved feelings about their children often have improved feelings about themselves as well. A child who performs well and receives recognition for the performance reflects well on his parents. The self-esteem of the parent may in turn be increased as they conclude, "If I have an okay kid. I must be okay too."

    The philosophy that "a child will lead them" significantly influences the AFY intervention approach. Instead of following the conventional belief that parents should be more responsible, and instead of attempting to change poor parents into good ones, who are subsequently expected to assume responsible parenting for their offspring, AFY has concluded that youths are often much more accessible and are much more open to overtures for service than are their parents. Therefore, AFY does not, as a rule—in the gang and school programs—initiate therapeutic work with parents. In many cases it would only delay work with the child and conceivably could prevent intervention from taking place altogether. However, every effort is made to obtain parental permission before or early in the service delivery process and to be available to parents when needed.

Once therapeutic work has been initiated, it is extremely rare that parents will terminate it. Far more frequently, they recognize the agency as a significant factor in the positive social change that has taken place in their child. Not only parents, but other adults, have expressed appreciation for "the help the kids are getting." Success of the child appears to be appreciated by parents because it validates the view that "we are not innately bad or inferior people." It expresses a hopefulness that, although circumstances have impaired our ability to become who we would have liked to be, our children have the potential to become who they want to be.

AFY's approach of beginning with the child has not been congruent with traditionalists at the Child and Adolescent Mental Health Division of the Hawaii Department of Health, who take the position that children are to be served exclusively top-down through their parents. Despite AFY's successes, and recognition, (supported by its many awards), as being uniquely qualified to work with the high-risk youth population, division bureaucrats continue to maintain their very limited and short-sighted perspective on how to reach the low-income, minority, high-risk child. Consequently, they don't reach them.

12. **Youths can be effectively helped without family intervention.** An axiom of traditional psychotherapy is the necessity of working with the family if the child is to be helped. Legally, financially, and for the sake of access, this nostrum makes

sense in many situations. Whether it is the best way to help the child is a separate matter. Youths who are in gangs and youths who are alienated from their parents, whatever the reasons, may be difficult to reach or, in fact, may be unreachable through parents. The mental health community, by maintaining its traditional and safe positions is denying many youths the opportunity of getting any help at all. From the traditional parental point of view, and that of those who make the policy decisions and the laws, it seems right that parents be involved in any program that addresses their child. It seems perfectly reasonable—except when the realities of parenthood are examined against the ideal. In a perfect world, parents are capable, loving, nurturing, supportive, and available to respond to their child's needs. In reality many parents are dysfunctional, abusive, manipulative, destructive, absent, and incapable of making decisions in the best interests of their children. To force such a parent on a child in order to "help" the child may only do additional damage. Access to the child is often easier to achieve by addressing the child directly and only involving parents as necessary. This isn't to say that parents should always be excluded, but neither is it to say that parents, as a matter of course, should always be included. At some point participation by motivated family members may enhance therapy, but within RT it isn't a requirement.

13. **It is best to work with multiple gangs in a community, especially rivals, if peace and stability are to occur.** Failure to do this may result in what AFY calls the Black Robe Syndrome. Just as AFY has learned that it is very difficult to work with one person outside of his/her friendship group, it understands that gangs don't operate in a vacuum either. If change occurs in one group and not in their rivals, the Black Robe Syndrome becomes applicable. The name derives from efforts by French Catholic missionaries to pacify Indian tribes in Canada. Their efforts ended in tragedy. Rivals to the pacified tribes exterminated them.

14. **Patience is a virtue.** Change doesn't occur overnight. It takes time for clients to feel good enough about themselves to develop the will to change. There is no silver bullet for reducing or eliminating crime and violence. It takes time to establish relationships, time to establish a climate for change, time to work through solutions to problems, and time to facilitate change. Simply being present and demonstrating unconditional positive regard, especially through the bad times, has its rewards.

    A former gang member who was also a drug user and alcoholic subsequently earned an Adult Friends for Youth Young Person of the Year Award. Upon receiving his award, before seven hundred people at our annual dinner/auction, he profusely thanked the staff member, who had always been there when he needed him, for being patient, and for being his "friend," no matter what and no matter how long it took.

    Patience and its companion, persistence, are not easy to master, even for the veteran practitioner. But AFY has found, in an era of quick-fix programs promising instant success, that when roots are planted deep, real change takes hold.

Chapter 4

Redirectional Therapy Practice

In the previous chapter, we presented a philosophy, or set of "truths," derived from experience, that we believe are prerequisites to helping gang members and other high-risk youths become emotionally healthy and constructive members of their communities and the society in which they live. Expressing a belief is only one part of the equation. Putting the belief into action is the second and most critical part of it.

Redirectional Therapy is a nonjudgmental, nondirective therapy. But, unlike Rogers, we are not purists in this regard. Unquestionably, we judge education to be a value and perceive it as a means for achieving individual freedom. The Redirectionalist also states personal opinions on any number of subjects, but, always by owning the message through an "I" statement and not presuming that what is "right" for him or her is right for everyone.

While the concepts "nonjudgmental" and "nondirective" may at first appear to be passive behaviors they are anything but passive. Great discipline and effort is required to explore and understand what the client is feeling and thinking, what his experiences have been, what he wants to achieve in life, and how he plans to get there. The greatest discipline of all is, after developing some sense of these things, not to behave like an adult who has the answers. The drive to solve problems quickly by providing answers and advice appears to be human nature. The Redirectionalist, on the other hand, practices patience, hypothesizing that when the client comes to his own conclusions he is more likely to own his decisions and take responsibility for them.

Society's approach to gang youths and others involved in destructive behaviors appears, most frequently, to be control and suppression. This translates into keeping them bottled up in jail or in their low-income, mostly minority neighborhoods, with little chance of escaping. The dream of "making it" through sports and music is promoted as a way of avoiding the reality that such opportunities come only to the fortunate few while the great majority will, without education, remain in the ghetto. The mission statement of AFY, or perhaps more importantly, its theme, is to "enhance the potential for *all* youths to achieve a rewarding life and become productive members of society." Without being melodramatic, but meaning every word of it, AFY strives to throw off the shackles of poverty by overcoming the lack of entitlement that many low-income minority youths feel. In this section we will discuss how we do it.

The practice of RT with gang youth usually occurs with the whole gang. Since gangs are mostly cohesive natural friendship groups with very loyal memberships, efforts to break them up by singling members out for treatment or punishment appear to be unrealistic and self-defeating. The hypothesis, "the fear of outside threats increases cohesion," is aptly applied to the gang.

As time goes by and the Redirectionalist becomes increasingly trusted and valued as a helping person, more time and work may be spent on some members than others and individual therapeutic relationships may emerge. As gang members become increasingly self-confident the cohesion of the gang tends to break down and members, no longer dependent on each other, go their separate ways.

The concepts that follow describe the work of the Redirectionalist.

1. **Turf.** Service is provided on the "turf" of the youths being served. Turf is defined as both a physical and psychological place. It is the geographic area, e.g., a neighborhood, housing

project, block, or territory, where members live or go to school, with which they identify and that they believe belongs to them, and where they feel that they are relatively safe. At school they may even carve out territory that they call their own and is their place to gather together, e.g., under the stairs, by the library, or at the gym. Fights may occur when rivals approach or attempt to cross "their" territory. It is the place where staff members can usually locate them. It is also their emotional comfort zone that includes their sense of how closely they can be physically approached. Approaches are most successful when conducted in a calm, open, nonthreatening, undemanding, and respectful manner. The Redirectionalist approaches the group as a potential guest in their home. To gain entry he must play by their rules. As a guest, the Redirectionalist is in no position to make demands or give advice. The Redirectionalist must always remember that the relationship lasts only as long as the "client" wants it to. Turf is also mobile. It is the personal space that surrounds and travels with the client and is different for every "client." It determines how close nonmembers are allowed to come.

2. **Referrals.** Requests to AFY for service may be initiated by any system including an individual, school, police, courts, parents, and even other groups, including gangs that are hoping to relieve tensions by getting help for their rivals. However, a decision to engage in a relationship can only be made between AFY, its staff, and the client. A referral is often very informal. A school may simply say, "See those kids hanging out over there? If you want them, they're yours. Good luck!" In one instance a girl came up to a staff member after a public housing event, and tugged at his shirt. When she had his attention, she proclaimed, "You help the boys. How come you never help us?" Needless to say, in a very short time we had a new group; a very tough group of girls with a fearsome reputation. Another group of girls refused to come to the office if they were present.

A television program conducted by the State of Hawaii Department of Education interviewed the group. In a very revealing interview the question was asked, "Why are so many of you not going to school?" One of the girls responded, "What's the point, if you think you aren't going to live long enough to graduate?" Others nodded in affirmation.

By reaching out to AFY they acknowledged that they were afraid of the direction that their lives had taken, that they wanted to change, and that they needed help if change was to happen. The young fourteen-year-old girl who first approached staff members and asked for help dramatically changed her life. Eight years later, in 2002, she was recognized as Adult Friends for Youth's Young Person of the Year (Her story, Sarah, appears in the "Stories from the Hood" chapter).

Because service is based on mutual agreement between AFY and its clients, it cannot be mandated by a third party, e.g., a court that implies the possible use of sanctions. A mandated service, as we have explained, would defeat AFY's principle of self-determination.

3. **Participation in the AFY program is fun and immediately rewarding.** The initial phase, where the relationship with the group is being formed, is also referred to as the seductive phase. This is a very pleasurable period where the group is being drawn into treatment by food, including treats such as chips and sodas, movies, sports, going to the beach, and cruising. The goal is to create a good feeling where the gang would rather be with AFY than look elsewhere for fun. While gratification is mostly gastronomical and sensory at first, it isn't long before it becomes more cerebral and emotional. Soon youths find that it feels good to have a person, whom they like and respect, listening to them, accepting them as equals in a give-and-take relationship, respecting them in turn, not judging them for their behavior, not talking down to them, and working with them and their peers to solve problems and plan for the future. Contact with

other staff members, including nonclinical staff members, is a bonus because they are treated the same way. Consequently, feelings of self-worth are reinforced.

4. **The Redirectionalist communicates care and love.** Statements that share feelings such as, "I love you," "I care about you," "You are important to me," and "I believe in you," have therapeutic value. One can only imagine how it must feel for someone who has suffered emotional deprivation and has truly never believed that they are loveable or capable of being loved to hear these words.

   A study conducted by social work students Adrian Abe, Patti May-Awaya, and Jan Yonemori at the University of Hawaii in 1988 revealed what adolescents said about how parents could demonstrate care and love to their children. Among the responses, each of which was repeated over and over again, were:

   a. Talk with your kids. Try to understand their point of view. Listen. Be fair. Be their friend and do things with them. Discuss things like you would with a friend.
   b. Give kids an opportunity to make decisions. If they feel that they are part of decision-making they won't rebel and sneak around.
   c. Be honest. Share things. If parents and adults are honest, kids will be honest. Don't act like you know everything. Give, once in a while.
   d. Don't be judgmental. Listen and try to understand. If you don't, kids won't tell you the truth. You won't hear the truth if a kid believes the truth will get him into trouble or result in disapproval.
   e. Trust your child.
   f. Children need to be allowed to fail once in a while without parents overreacting. They need to feel that they don't have to be perfect to be loved, and that if they fail it doesn't make them a bad person.

g. Parents ought to give their opinions through "I" messages rather than telling teenagers what they should or shouldn't do. Parents often have a different perspective because their experiences have been different. It doesn't help to remind us of the way things were. Things are different today.
h. There is too much quarreling. The world would be a better place without it.
i. Make your children feel wanted. Tell them that you love them.
j. Don't yell. Talk calmly to your children and they will do the same.
k. Adults should be more humble and try to reduce the stress in their lives, e.g., "If you are more relaxed you won't be taking your problems out on me."
l. Don't make future plans for your kids and expect them to be what you want them to be.

Many of these responses are reflected in Redirectional Therapy.

5. **Redirectional Therapy is nonjudgmental.** The term is synonymous with unconditional positive regard. Clients are accepted unconditionally, without regard to past or present behaviors, culture, or beliefs. It accepts young people with all of their warts and without preconditions. The message is, "I care about you because you have value." As the client begins to see him/herself as having value, a perception that "I am precious, life is precious, and other people are precious," begins to emerge. As we discussed in the philosophy chapter, Berne labeled this emerging behavior as the "plus-plus," or "I'm okay, you're okay" life position. We often find gang members, when we initiate service, to be in the very dangerous "minus-minus" ("I'm not okay, you're not okay") position, or the extreme suicidal ("I'm not okay, you're okay") position. The "suicide by cop" phenomenon appears to have emerged from these feelings.
6. **Redirectional Therapy is nondirective.** The Redirectionalist's opinions are expressed authentically by giving "I" messages. He/

she doesn't give advice by telling other people how they should or shouldn't live their lives. Instead of admonishing clients with "shoulds," "shouldn'ts," "oughts," and "ought nots" the Redirectionalist helps clients assess their unique situations and work out solutions that they believe are in their best interests. On the other hand, the Redirectionalist may share what he/she might personally do in a given situation. Since the helper is a trusted person, the point of view that is shared may influence the client. This principle is based on the belief that sharing how you believe you would behave can provide insight, but you can't expect others to be you. The Redirectionalist may also engage in an exploration of options from which choices may be made.

There are exceptions to the nondirective principle. Where health and safety issues are at stake, direct intervention by the therapist may be required in the moment. An example would be breaking up a fight, or removal of a group from a potential conflict. On numerous occasions the Honolulu Police Department and school security officers have acknowledged the influence of AFY staff members with their groups and have backed off when staff members intervened in tense situations.

7. **The Redirectionalist is empathic.** This principle coincides with nondirective practice. It recognizes that each person has his/her own set of internal references, and, as much as one is able, an attempt is made to understand the experiences and perceptions that comprise the client's world. However, although the therapist may attempt to understand a problem by looking at it as if he/she were the client, the "as if" factor still remains. He/she is not the client. RT understand that it is difficult to put yourself in someone else's shoes, and, therefore, that the art of empathy takes ceaseless practice.
8. **Active listening.** The ability to empathize requires the therapist to be present with the client. It means listening to what is being said and understanding the meaning of both verbal and nonverbal messages. The Redirectionalist is alert to the signals of

the environment/turf being trod upon, and attempts to validate what is being communicated.

In structured individual and group therapy sessions with gangs and gang members, traditional modes of validation appear to work well. They include summarizing, paraphrasing, evaluating, and repeating words for clarity. They send the message that, "I care about what you are saying and I'm trying to get it right. If I don't understand, please correct me." Getting things right may be easier said than done, especially early in a relationship. Rather than working at an understanding, it may be easier, out of frustration, for the client to just give up and say, "Forget about it." The persistence of the therapist may help overcome resistance, but care is required to not push too hard. The active listener may also be hearing/feeling that the message is "back off, this is not the time to pursue the issue." There is always another day. Active listening appears to be at least as much feeling as hearing.

Instinct, intuition, gut feeling, experience, whatever you want to call it, may require an immediate response that leaves no room for validation. That is when you tell the group, when you perceive danger, what you want from them, e.g., "Get in the van now," without discussing it. The discussion can come later.

9. **Modeling legal and healthy behaviors.** It is not illegal for adults to smoke cigarettes or drink alcohol. Clinical staff members may engage in these behaviors on their own time, but not, however, in the presence of clients. The rule of thumb is to avoid engaging in any behaviors that impair or have a significant potential to impair health, including the physical and emotional health of others. Therefore, belligerent or angry outbursts suggesting that violence is permissible would be counter to this principle. The Redirectionalist is responsible for consciously using him/herself as a model and professional helper whenever in the company of clients. This principle can also be applied to protect the Redirectionalist if pressure to engage in unhealthy or ille-

gal behaviors is brought to bear by clients. In other words, the therapist can always fall back on the agency's position.

10. **Encouraging new social and activity experiences: The Six-Point Plan.** Youths living in low-income communities tend to have very limited experiences outside of their immediate neighborhood. This includes both lack of familiarity with other neighborhoods and people beyond certain geographic boundaries, and a limited range of activities to which they have been exposed and have access. People with whom they have contact are most likely to look and behave like them, and come from similar ethnic, cultural, and economic backgrounds. Travel is limited. Athletic activities that are taken for granted by middle-class youths may not be available to low-income young people. Youth sports such as soccer and baseball that depend on volunteer coaches are often nonexistent. Tennis and golf, which are perceived as more upper-class activities, and especially golf, which requires expensive equipment and fees to play, are generally not pursued. Limited knowledge of and experience with the wider world often generates misperceptions, fear, anger, and hostility. In our office when a Polynesian group and a Filipino group encountered each other they were surprised to learn that they both liked the same music. This simple exchange of information was a humanizing experience for both groups. The Six-Point Plan is a means for broadening the experiences of groups. It provides a guideline for both staff members and groups to participate in a variety of activities. It is recommended that groups plan and implement at least one activity in each category, annually. Of course it is not compulsory to do so. The six categories are:

    a. SOCIAL ACTIVITIES. This includes parties, eating out, movies, going to the beach and parks, cookouts and camping, attending concerts, going to the theater, singing, music, arts and crafts, acting/drama, dancing, storytelling, and similar activities.

b. RECREATION AND SPORTS. Examples are hiking, swimming, playing team sports (including inter-group competition), bowling, pool/billiards, skating, bicycling, ping-pong, boxing, martial arts, shooting marbles, skateboarding, canoe paddling, body boarding and surfing, video games, active and quiet group games, fishing, and attending sporting events, to name a number of activities that we have used. Many of our groups consist of Pacific Islander populations, including Samoans, Tongans, Hawaiians, and Micronesians, who have an affinity for rugby. We have built on this interest using the expertise of our staff in the sport and developed an annual seven-a-side rugby tournament that has included not only our groups, but teams from as far away as New Zealand, Canada, and Pennsylvania. Girls competed for the first time in 2007. The emphasis is on sportsmanship and sociability. Social activities enable players to get to know each other more intimately and to break down barriers. By the end of the two-day tournament players from various Hawaiian communities (even where rivalries have existed) and distant places, are no longer strangers to each other. They come away having learned something positive about people who look different and come from backgrounds different from their own.

c. EDUCATION. This is a big thing with AFY. We promote it as a means for our clients to acquire individual freedom. To advance this goal we work with students and their schools to solve academic problems. Staff members act as advocates with teachers, counselors, and administrators. We also provide tutoring and help prepare students for General Education Diploma (GED) examinations. We also conduct group visits to college campuses, help prepare college applications, have admissions counselors as guest speakers at group sessions, and arrange for scholarships. In an endeavor to meet the needs of students who have dropped out, we established an alternative school program through the Hawaii Department of Education (DOE). The program known as Competency-Based Education, or C-Base, is conducted through the Department's Adult Community School, and leads to a high school diploma. It is conducted by clinical staff members and wraps the clinical program around an academic program. We also provide tutoring for these students. The graduation rate in 2007 was 91 percent, which was 27 percent higher than the statewide graduation rate. Tests, grades and diplomas are tamper-proof, since they are administered and awarded by the DOE. Besides visiting college campuses, we visit, as part of the general education experience, museums, courts, prisons, trade schools, libraries, and upper-income communities. Travel outside of students' comfort zones satisfies curiosity and provides a wider perspective on the community and the world, and to what they can aspire.

d. EMPLOYMENT AND CAREERS. When students* begin to believe that they have the potential for a future that is worth living they begin to look beyond the here-and-now. Excitement begins to grow about planning for the future to which they aspire. Groups begin to explore careers that interest the members, and to look at the preparation that is needed to achieve their goals. Discussions may involve apprenticeships, college, and even the military, as means for getting to where they want to go. Groups have even gone to downtown Honolulu to observe how people dress for business. In one exercise they attempt to guess the occupations of people they observe by the way they dress. They then approach the person to find out what they actually do for a living. Group members prepare for this exercise by thinking through how they should dress, and how to present themselves in order to

---

* Clients in therapeutic groups are often referred to as students even when they are not in school. Staff find it more comfortable and less pejorative than the term, "client."

obtain a friendly response. Role-plays in appropriate dress are conducted to prepare students for this experience and also to prepare them for job interviews. Videotaping of these role-plays allows students to critique themselves and each other. In one experience a gang followed the construction of a bank building and explored various tasks associated with it. They were amazed at the range of occupations involved, including financing, architecture, drafting, engineering, law, and the construction trades. In addition to learning how to prepare for job interviews, students practice filling out application forms—sometimes at the employment site or at job fairs. They also learn to read want-ads in newspapers and online. Money management, which includes opening checking and savings accounts, understanding how credit cards work, the concept of interest both from the perspectives of earning it and paying it (particularly credit-card interest), and the value of saving as a means for achieving long-term goals, is explored. Staff members also assist students in getting to job interviews.

e. CULTURE AND RELIGION. A perception of cultures and religions that concludes, "My beliefs and practices are okay, but yours are not okay," contains, we believe, the seeds of destruction. Shared social experiences that include discussions, music, dance, athletics, and food—especially food—provide opportunities to break down barriers and enhance relationships. One Samoan group touched its own roots by learning Samoan dances that they subsequently performed in public. These performances also accomplished the objective of establishing a connection between gang kids and audiences that began to appreciate them as decent, talented people. A Filipino group shopped for, prepared, and ate food from various cultures, learning more about each one through the experience. A number of gang leaders were brought together for lunch and discussion in an upscale neighborhood. Three goals were achieved through this event. Food and a shared experience helped them appreciate their commonalities. For the first time, many of them ordered food off of a printed menu. They were introduced to a community that was as alien to them as a foreign country. Examples of activities engaged in by groups include attending church/temple services of other religions, visiting art exhibits and museums, visits to historical sites, exploring superstitions, and ghost walks.

f. COMMUNITY SERVICE. This is an area of activity that we don't want groups to feel obligated to do. Rather, when they are ready, we would like them to engage in it as a way to experience the feeling of making a contribution to their community. Community service demonstrates that they have the power to do something that helps other people. It has enormous therapeutic value because it contributes so much to feelings of competency and self-worth. Projects in which AFY groups have participated include:

- Graffiti paint-outs. (When gangs clean up graffiti in their neighborhood it tends to stay off.) This result is much different than when an outside group comes in. In one housing project, three generations of a gang painted out graffiti on a building that they had marked up for many years. After repainting the building, it remained graffiti-free for several years.
- Picking up trash and sweeping down streets.
- Cleaning and painting a children's park and dedicating it back to the children. (Shortly thereafter, the city put in all new equipment.) The park, which was notorious for drive-by shootings, became a peaceful place to gather.
- Voter registration. This was also a fundraiser for one group that was paid for its services through the Lt. Governor's Office.
- Presenting talks. Gang members have spoken to as many as four thousand fifth- and sixth-grade students at AFY's

annual Student Transition Conventions about the difficulties they've experienced in their lives, and how, with help, they have changed. They have also talked to classes of college students, participated in numerous forums that have included social workers, nurses, and educators, and appeared on television. These presentations have occurred over many years.

- Entertaining and presenting gifts to sick children at the Shriners' Hospital, and to the elderly at nursing homes.
- Cleaning out the ponds and canals at the Polynesian Cultural Center.

11. **Food as therapy.** Food is recognized as a basic human need and therapeutic instrument, and is used liberally. It resolves hunger, provides nutrition, helps members relax, contributes to socializing and bonding, is recreational, and is a source of pleasure. Food helps people feel content and happy. It contributes to a sense of well-being. For adolescents, who consume energy at prodigious rates, it is the fuel that maintains their energy level. Not only do we provide it at all group sessions, but we offer meals for youths and staff members when they have been involved in something special, such as a presentation or a television interview. For budget purposes food is included as a therapeutic program expense. Most of the kids with whom we work are poor and the food that we provide often satisfies hunger. Expecting them to concentrate on group business while hungry makes no sense. In many cultures the offering of food conveys respect and love, and that is the effect it appears to have on our kids. We find that it is the best way to break down barriers when we initiate service to a group. It also helps to break down barriers when conducting mediations. Some groups, when we first begin with them, have been known to affectionately call the agency Adult Friends for Food.
12. **Self-determination.** The practice of self-determination is fundamental to developing an awareness of personal freedom and

power, and the responsibility that accompanies it. As group members engage in decision-making, the sense that they can control and influence their lives is established. This is a vastly different experience from being told how to live your life by authority figures whose interests may be different from your own. With the euphoria of freedom to make decisions also comes the burden of responsibility. There is no one to blame for the outcomes except yourself. Conversely, when compelled to do the bidding of others there may be resentment, little or no commitment, little or no sense of responsibility, and a propensity to lay the blame for failure on others.

13. **Nonintrusive, attentive style.** There is a lot to be said about the impact of style. It is the way that we present ourselves to other people and the way that they perceive us. Through acculturation an AFY staff style has emerged over time. It can best be described, although somewhat ambiguously, as laid-back. It conveys being easygoing, not rushing, not pushy, and not intrusive. The Redirectionalist is willing to take time to develop relationships and to achieve change. The therapist pays attention to the client and the client's environment. The beginning of a relationship is a learning process about wants and needs of both the group, as an entity, and each individual. Relationships are given time to mature.

A "Do as I say, I know best," attitude may work for a coach. It doesn't work for the Redirectionalist, who is striving to achieve self-determination and personal responsibility for behavior, and in a situation where punishment and dismissal from the program are not options.

The dress of staff members also reflects style. It doesn't draw attention to the clinician. Jewelry and fragrances are minimized. Clothing does not emulate that of gang members. For want of a better description, we refer to it as adult-casual. Athletic clothes are worn for sports, swimsuits for the beach, and business attire for meetings and public gatherings. Dress is appropriate to the occasion and not sloppy or idiosyncratic.

Chapter 5

Mediation

AFY never had a plan for its staff members to become mediators in gang disputes. It was one of those things that emerged from necessity. We saw the need for mediation between rival groups early on, and, at first, attempted to utilize professional mediators. When offered the opportunity, groups with whom we were working were willing to engage in the process only because they trusted us, but it became apparent, once mediations began, that this trust did not extend to the mediators. By the very nature of professional mediation, focus was on objectivity and neutrality, but for our clients it was too cold and formal. Relationships with AFY, on the other hand, were expected to be warm and friendly. One obvious distinction was that disputants in mediation are typically not in a therapeutic relationship and do not expect support and nurturing. Further, mediators cannot be expected to have the therapeutic skills required to develop the rapport that work with this population requires, and even if they did, wouldn't have the time necessary to establish that rapport.

We also experienced that schools, when they brought gangs together to resolve disputes, inevitably and flagrantly misused the term "mediation." As the term is commonly applied it refers to a neutral third-party helping, with the consent of the disputants, to find a mutually acceptable resolution to the issues being disputed.

AFY was appalled to find that what schools called mediation was, most often, simply laying down the law to the students involved in the conflict. Two separate incidents at two different schools illustrate our experience. In both situations groups in conflict were brought together under the guise of mediation and were read the riot act by the "mediators," who laid down the consequences if they didn't "straighten out." The exclamation point to the school's position was made by the presence of police officers on both occasions. No effort was made to determine the cause of the conflict, nor to work with the groups toward a resolution.

At one meeting, AFY was actually prepared to conduct the mediation, and in fact had initiated it through the school. However, when staff members arrived, the principal took over. On the plus side, after she had her say, the officers (about six) refrained from adding anything. Subsequently, we were able to save they day by conducting the mediation that we had planned. Both groups pleasantly surprised us. They demonstrated enormous resiliency in their willingness to move on after being dressed down by the principal. We surmised that they were accustomed to the way schools conducted such matters and just let it wash over them.

The process that followed demonstrated that our approach worked. It was especially interesting because while one of the groups was a client the other was not. Yet, by reputation, the non-client group also trusted us to be fair. The event that precipitated the mediation was an all-out street fight the day before.

It appeared that at least one condition to successful mediation was present, e.g., "a genuine desire on the part of the parties to find a positive solution to the dispute." However, it violated another condition, resolution "through the help of an independent, neutral third-party not connected with any of the involved parties." We've found, subsequently, that it is possible to violate this principle as long as it is apparent that no favoritism to any party is being displayed. AFY's role is to allow each party to meet separately and formulate its grievances toward the other party, come together and present their grievance on blackboards or display paper, discuss, one by one, the legitimacy of their grievances, and, finally, come to an agreement on the manner whereby concerns can be resolved.

The role of staff members is not, in the traditional sense, what is meant by an "independent, neutral third party," but if staff members—and usually there are at least two staff members participating—perform as "independent, neutral third parties" and have the benefit of a trusting relationship, we have concluded that the process can be very productive. Unquestionably, staff members must have the professional discipline to pull it off.

In our second experience, hostilities that had been brewing for weeks between two well-established gangs finally exploded at a high school football game. The blow-up was so explosive that it threatened to end the football season of the school where the fight occurred. The school administration was traumatized, not only by the fight itself, but by the recognition that it had a serious gang problem on its hands. At the time, AFY had no experience with either of the groups.

The school immediately reacted and called a "mediation." Again, "mediation" was a terrible misnomer. This time, in addition to a strong police presence, parents were called in, and representatives of the district superintendent attended. School officials and the police, in turn, laid down the consequences of any future misbehavior. Intimidation, not mediation, was the order of the day. AFY contended that more than a one-time lecture would be required if a long-lasting resolution was to be achieved. No one had thought much beyond this single flexing of school and police muscle.

AFY proceeded to ask if we could speak to the parents and each of the groups separately. This was agreed to, and, fortunately, we achieved the primary objective of an agreement between the groups for a cooling-off period. It was anticipated that the peace would be short lived without longer-term services to both groups. However, when AFY broached the subject of compensation for starting work with the groups it was greeted with blank stares from the district reps. In a subsequent meeting with school officials, including vice-principals, counselors, and other personnel, a plea was made to AFY for help. We argued that we would need some financial support from the school. Attendees said that they would see what they could do. Since they pleaded that they were in a crisis situation and needed help now, AFY relented and immediately initiated work with both groups. Financial support was never forthcoming, and, subsequently, the principal, who didn't attend the meeting, expressed resentment that AFY even raised the need for funds. Services were provided to those groups and their successors for over five years without a dime from the school.

AFY's position has always been that it responds to the needs of the youths, and, once it begins service, continues as long as they want it. This policy has often stretched AFY's resources to the breaking point, especially when a school refuses to help.

In the past, schools seeking mediation were, all too frequently, focused only on the here-and-now. They wanted first aid to stop the bleeding, but failed to commit to a cure. Consequently, they continued to experience a chain of crises. Fortunately, over time, as AFY has demonstrated success, schools have been willing to commit resources and stronger relationships have been forged.

Mediation, for the most part, is an activity that AFY sees as part of a process. This is not, usually, the way others see it. Much too frequently it is perceived as an isolated quick-fix event. Since AFY's philosophy rests on a belief that long-term services lead to long-term solutions, many times it finds itself engaged well beyond the mediation. The payoff occurs when fighting stops and productive behaviors, including improved attendance and grades, begin.

Unlike professional mediators we do have a personal interest in the parties to the dispute and our interest may go on for several years. Fortunately, the desire for change in most cases is mutual.

Over time, most of our clients begin to believe in their worth. Consequently, they expect to be treated with respect and as equals in relationships. When they experience outsiders, e.g., mediators, media people, and researchers, who talk down to them or treat them as mere subjects, what they refer to as "lab rats," they deeply resent it and clam up. On the other hand, if time is taken to get to know them—the Hawaii term is "talk story"—through relaxed, warm interaction before getting down to business, they tend to respond openly and congenially. They absolutely reject anyone who lectures to them, unless that person is someone who they respect, and then only when they know they've screwed up.

McKay Schwenke, Malakai Maumalanga, and Debbie Spencer-Chun, who have conducted many of our mediations, provided insights into what they do and what works for them. When the school conducts a "mediation," it is all about the exercise of authority. This contrasts sharply with AFY's relationship with schools and students. AFY has no legal authority and, thus, no official power. Whatever influence or power it has emerges through the acknowledgment of its success by clients and institutions.

Mac and Debbie believe that preparation is the key to a successful mediation. Both individual group members, who may have triggered the problem, and their groups, must be engaged even before getting the groups together in a room.

Although mediations are usually conducted between groups with whom we are already working, sometimes, as noted, they are conducted where we are only working with one group, and at other times where we have no therapeutic relationship with either group. Mediations may also be conducted between individuals or factions of the same gang. Not infrequently, groups will be asked to send representatives to a mediation rather than having the whole group present. This may occur if the groups are too large, or if a large gathering is perceived as counterproductive. "Representative mediation," however, has a major drawback. Sometimes representatives don't feel they have the authority to make commitments for their friends, and may need to go back and discuss proposals before continuing with the mediation. Many groups do not have a clear line of authority. Members often see themselves as equals among equals. In that sense their groups are pure democracies.

The initial phase of the mediation requires processing, with each disputant, their perceptions of the incident and or history of the incident. Discovery often involves a "venting session." If it takes place on the same day as the conflict, "the kids are still pretty heated up and are looking to get back at the other side," according to Mac. Tensions are running high and violent responses are being expressed. The clinician then has to filter out the facts, which involves talking to the individuals who were directly involved, and talking to the group about what they heard and saw and how they became involved. Not uncommonly, the group only knows what they have been told, and that is what they are reacting to. The facts, as they are revealed, may tell a different story. The past also must be uncovered. The group's history with the other side also plays into the presenting conflict. This beginning phase may take an hour, a day, or longer. Nonjudgmental listening and patience are required of the mediator(s).

It is also important to find out if other people or groups may be stirring the pot. Modern technology generates new problems. With cell phones, computers, YouTube, etc., people are taking pictures, and it isn't long before a fight is all over the Internet, and people are involved who weren't even present at the precipitating incident. Mediators, consequently, may find themselves dealing not only with the youths who were present, but also, their friends, family, and others who insinuate themselves into the issue.

The mediators always ask, "Now that we have examined what happened, where do you want to go with it?" When payback is still on their minds, food often tends to calm emotions and ease tensions. Mediation can't take place until the disputants agree to it. This is the all-important first step.

Style is important. Mediators are relaxed and not pushy or demanding. They proceed at the pace of the disputants. By the time the groups arrive at phase two, the actual mediation, they are usually motivated to reach a solution. They are tired of being afraid, of fighting, getting in trouble at school, and of being arrested.

Each group presents its grievances and has the opportunity to challenge the other side. Eventually, a clearer picture of what actually happened begins to emerge. For example, a group may deny they mobbed someone, but during the mediation it may come out that it was four against one. Then comes the acknowledgement, "Yeah, I guess we wen mob 'em."

When they sit down and eat together, following the mediation session, barriers tend to be broken down further. They find it pleasant to be in a relaxed social setting rather than to be confrontational and angry.

While AFY emphasizes the importance of relationships to the successful mediation process, it has also had success mediating with groups that are not its clients. An apparent contradiction arises. In one case where we mediated between students attending Farrington High School and a group living in Ewa Beach (communities over 15 miles distant from one another), neither of whom were clients at the time, it worked this way:

1. We were able to pluck the Farrington group out of Ewa Beach and away from a standoff with the police when the police allowed us to intercede, and because the boys knew by reputation that AFY helps kids. In this tense situation our reputation with both the youths and the police served us well.
2. The nonjudgmental attitude, style and personality of the staff enabled them to enter phase one with both groups, which involved a day of discussion prior to the actual mediation. Feelings were soothed to the point that when the groups came together they were ready to resolve their dispute.
3. Phase two proceeded quickly and concluded the mediation successfully.

    Deb and Mac, when conducting a mediation between their groups, make it a point to meet with the other staff members' group, so that the groups understand that they are not taking sides and that during the mediation they will be neutral. It is necessary to communicate that they are working together and that they care equally for both groups. They share that they don't want anyone to get hurt or get arrested. The mediation process is not a competition to determine if one group is right or wrong, but rather is a mutual effort to get at the facts and achieve a resolution agreeable to the parties. The roles assumed by the staff members during the mediation confirm that they meant what they said regarding their neutrality. Physically, staff members position themselves in the middle of the room—not with either group. Everything that they do or say sends the message that they are Adult Friends for Youth staff and that they are concerned for everyone. Questions are never accusatory. It is helpful to the final resolution, when the groups have had a history of trust and sense of fairness with AFY, and have come to expect it.

Staff members also follow up with their colleague's group to enhance their relationship. By establishing these relationships it allows them to intervene in subsequent shaky situations with their colleague's group. Staff members are conscious of themselves as members of a team invested in a common purpose that requires them to support each other. There is no room for an arrogant staff member who believes she or he knows it all. AFY staff strives to achieve a humble approach to clients that conveys humility, treats clients with respect and dignity, and believes in their capacity to live successful and accomplished lives.

We have been asked, "Do groups feel abandoned or resentful during mediations when the clinician whom they see as their advocate assumes a neutral position?" Deb doesn't believe this is a problem. She responded, "When we go back to our groups they understand that we are really trying to help them by resolving the conflict." Mac added, "Sometimes groups actually get along with each other, but one or two members, because of their actions, raise tensions. Other members may want to get the problem resolved as soon as possible, because if they don't it means that someone on the other side who has become a friend becomes an enemy again, and that is not what they want to happen. Even if they aren't exactly friends they are 'cool' with each other and don't want to be forced into a fight. Mediation can be the face saving means for avoiding what they don't really want to happen anyway."

A typical mediation will proceed as follows:

1. A mediator explains to each group, separately, what will happen and informs them that he/she understands that they've agreed to try and resolve their dispute, and that is the reason he/she is meeting with them. Mediator thanks them for their agreement to mediate.
2. Each group will select a spokesperson who will explain what his group believes happened. The other side will then have the opportunity to respond.
3. Groups are asked to respect statements of the other side even if they don't agree with them, because they will have their turn to respond, and will expect the other side to listen to them. If someone jumps in out of turn they are reminded that they will have their chance.
4. They are informed that they can disagree with the other side, and when it is their turn they will have the opportunity to present their side of the story.
5. The discussion goes back and forth until there is an agreement on the facts. AFY encourages participants to be honest with their feelings, and to say what they want to say, but to avoid using offensive language. AFY encourages empathy by helping members understand how they would feel if someone said or did something that was offensive, or "gave attitude."

It is not uncommon for confrontations and fights to occur because of rumors, sometimes spread with the intention of causing harm. We attempt to help groups understand this phenomenon. On one occasion two girls were identified as spreading rumors. They were brought into the mediation and questioned about what they had said, and confronted with the damage that they had done. Both groups, after the facts were separated from the falsehoods, apologized to each other. They held the girls accountable for their acts and admonished them to not repeat their behavior. There were not so subtle hints that they might not get off so easily if their actions were repeated. After the air was cleared, the groups went out together to engage in their really favorite pastime—eating.

Deb and Mac observed that it's harder for the group walking into the mediation than it is for the group that is already seated. "We will ask each group, before they come together, whether they are ready, and ask the group already in the room not to slouch, but to sit up and not give attitude when the other group enters."

Deb commented, "On rare occasions someone will get upset and walk out of the room. Since there is more than one staff member present, the one who knows him best can follow him out, calm him down, and help him return to the session."

We've found that gang members are not offended by being labeled at-risk. They see this as being honest. Because they often feel helpless to change the situation in which they find themselves, more often than not, they appear to welcome AFY's involvement. The mediation process offers hope of resolving problems, and changes feelings of helplessness to hopefulness. The process is empowering. It provides a sense of accomplishment and the understanding that they have the capacity to solve problems. We know that AFY's mediator role has been appreciated by the thanks we have received from disputants, the schools that have been helped, and other observers. U.S. Attorney Ed Kubo and the Leeward School District acknowledged the significant work we did in bringing the Ewa Beach–Farrington High School conflict to a successful conclusion without anyone getting hurt and/or arrested.

The fearlessness that staff members exhibit, whether it's reaching out to a gang, engaging them in a therapeutic relationship, or conducting a mediation, appears to come from a belief that they belong in the situation. While others may be frightened by the idea of interacting with a gang, going into a housing project, or being in a hostile environment, AFY staff members have shared that they cloak themselves in the belief that they know what they are doing and it is for a good purpose. It helps them transcend the potential dangers. After two decades of work, no staff member has been physically harmed by a gang member, whether client or not.

They find, also, that certain behaviors, that include humor and patience, really help. Pushy, aggressive, controlling behaviors that may be appropriate in competitive enterprises, or in controlled environments, are antithetical to Redirectional Therapy and would, in our experience, be counterproductive. In mediation, even when time appears to be of the essence, the Redirectionalist attempts to be calm and deliberate. It is also imperative in mediations that staff have confidence and trust in each other.

Are mediations always successful? Unfortunately, they are not. There is still that pesky 20 percent.

Part II –

The Young People

Chapter 6

Stories from the Hood

Adult Friends for Youth looks at gang members through a lens that is distinctly different from the popular perception of who gang members are and what to do about them. To the mainstream, they are a faceless and nameless breed apart; not quite fully realized human beings who, consequently, can be treated harshly, without compassion and without guilt. The Nazi definition of subhumans or "*untermenchen*" comes to mind. However, in our view, Pogo cartoonist Walt Kelly, who is popularly quoted as saying, "We have met the enemy and he is us," got it right. Kids in gangs are us. Mostly, they have become who they are not because they are less human, but because of their life experiences. AFY has demonstrated that as their experiences are altered their perceptions of who they are and who they can become are also altered.

This chapter will open a window and reveal who these gang members really are and what formed them. It will, hopefully, pull down the wall of indifference that divides "them" from "us." It will look at their potential for change and how the persistent application of Redirectional Therapy helped them become the people that they really wanted to become. Above all, we hope we can convey the humanity that exists within even the seemingly hardest cases.

Masa

Masa was hard core all they way. He once described himself as a "straight-up menace to society." He said, "Growing up on the streets, I walked the walk, talked the talk and no one was going to stand in my way." Even as a gang leader with a reputation as a fighter to be greatly feared, he felt that when it came right down to it, he was alone. He wrote, "Everything I did was on my own. I fought the world alone. I raised myself because both my parents were too busy working. I taught myself how to live by the law of the streets without thinking about my future or my education."

The gang eventually moderated his feelings of loneliness. "We were all in the same boat—all had the same problems, so we called ourselves The Family. This second family of mine showed me how it felt to be loved."

Sid first met Masa at a restaurant when he was fourteen years old. His reputation as a street fighter preceded him. Sid recalled his impressions, "I expected a tough-looking kid with an aggressive attitude. Instead I was introduced to a tall wiry boy with a warm smile who looked more like a poet than a fighter. He was well-spoken and polite."

"Masa reflected, in our interview many years later, that he took on different personas depending on the person with whom he was relating. The notion that you can't judge a book by its cover certainly applied to him. It was abundantly clear, however, that he was smart and a leader. He exuded an easy confidence and the ability to adapt to his surroundings. We talked comfortably with each other even though I was his senior by many years.

"The nineteen years that have passed since our first meeting have been a roller-coaster ride for him. My interview was conducted when he was thirty-three years old."

Masa arrived in Hawaii from Tonga at the age of two. When he was four years of age his family moved into the tough Kalihi immigrant community, populated mostly by Filipinos and Samoans. The family was fairly typical of most immigrants. They came to Hawaii for a better life and especially better educational opportunities for their children. Masa said that education was the one thing that his parents always emphasized. Eventually, there were five children. He was second-oldest and the oldest male. He had three sisters and a younger brother.

One of his fondest early memories upon arriving in Hawaii was eating hamburgers and ice cream. He said he craved them every day, and his parents indulged him.

School, at first, was difficult. He was bullied by the Samoans because he was Tongan and felt that he didn't fit in anywhere. He was picked on from kindergarten to third grade. When he was in the third grade he told himself that he wasn't going to let anyone else pick on him and started to get into fights after school. The problem escalated and before long he was fighting everywhere—in class, in the library—it made no difference.

"My friends at that time," he said, "were the smaller kids. I would go after the bullies that picked on them. I protected them."

At about the same time he began to socialize with some high school boys who hung out at a wall near his house. The group called themselves the King's Guards. He became a member of the gang when he was only a third-grader. He was their lookout. He also hid weapons in various places for them. The neighborhood was seen as a dangerous place. They had enemies in an enclave surrounding a park across the street and at an adjacent public housing project. Weapons that included "knives, rocks, bottles, and sticks" were stashed where the gang "cruised."

Eventually many of the King's Guards, including the leader, ended up going to prison, and the group just disappeared. When it fell apart Masa switched loyalties. He claimed the Crip blue rag of a Polynesian gang that was fighting his enemies in the neighborhood across the street.

Masa commented that gangs were a fact of life when he was growing up. He had cousins who were in other gangs in other neighborhoods.

If you were in a social group in a low-income neighborhood you were almost by definition in a gang. He said that in his experience gang members got into fights, drank, smoked, and did drugs at an early age. In the environment in which he grew up these were normal behaviors (Sutherland and Cressey referred to behaviors that are acceptable in a subculture but not acceptable in the greater culture as "differential association," and that they may be necessary for survival). "Violence is a norm for these kids," Masa observed. He said that he thrived on the violence, and that over time it became an addiction. When I asked him if he was ever afraid, he replied that he had no fear.

While growing up, he was seldom at home. He didn't have the TV cartoon experience. In retrospect he said he missed doing the kinds of things that other elementary school-age kids did.

All through elementary school, despite the gang-banging, Masa's grades were good, so good, in fact, that he was placed in gifted and talented classes. In seventh and eighth grades his school work began to fall apart. By the time he entered ninth grade his grades had fallen completely off the cliff and he went from gifted and talented to being placed in the Special Motivation Program—a very long fall.

Between seventh and eighth grades he found his fit with a gang of Filipino boys in the enclave that comprised gangs he formerly fought with. His family had moved into the area. He was the only Tongan member. Other Tongans saw his membership in the Filipino gang as a betrayal.

The members of this new gang, ironically, tested each other with a form of initiation, but subsequently, did not jump in new members. The rationale was that the group was involved in so many fights that they could find out who was "down" by observing how they did in actual fights. Since they were already "battle-tested," any other test would have been redundant. Potential members were also expected to fit in and have the "right attitude." Failure to possess the required profile resulted in rejection. Failure to achieve acceptance meant you could no longer hang out. If you didn't get the message you would be driven off. Several boys thus rejected became members of rival gangs.

The Family grew to become one of the largest gangs in Honolulu. As members moved to other islands, affiliates were established in those places. Mainland affiliations, especially in Las Vegas, also developed. The thinking in local law enforcement circles is that Hawaii is being contaminated by mainland gangs. In truth, movement is along a two-way street.

Masa described his parents as strict and his father, who would hit him with anything that was handy, as "old-school." He recalled being beaten on his butt with a two-by-four when he was only in the first grade. He said he hurt so much that he couldn't sit down. His mother tried, unsuccessfully, to intervene but his father blamed her lack of discipline as the reason Masa stole candy from a store in the first place.

As the oldest boy, he was also held responsible for any bad behavior of the other children. He felt this was unfair and it made him very angry. The physical punishment from his father continued until he was in the seventh grade. After he suffered a beating he would go out and find someone he could take it out on.

Despite the beatings, he defended his father's behavior. "He didn't know any other way. It was the way he was raised. He was different with me than with my brother and the girls. Much of the discipline I experienced was because I was expected to be the head of the family one day. My father never told me that he loved me until I was going to prison. The year was 2001. He thought I would be gone for a long time. When he said that to me I was shocked. I never heard anything like that. Expressions of affection were not something I experienced in my family. I never saw my mother and father hold hands or hug each other. Cultural tradition wouldn't allow it."

Masa's family always had high expectations for him, too many, he felt. His grandfather had been the head of the extended family. It was subsequently a role that was passed down to his father, and upon his death it will pass to Masa. It will be his responsibility to attend all the funerals and other family functions. "It's just too much," he says.

His family had very limited financial resources even though both his father and mother worked very hard. He was resentful that families portrayed on television had so much while his family had so little (an awareness of a world of plenty from which gang members and their families were excluded, and consequential resentment and anger, is a theme that ran through several interviews). A factor that contributed to the family's limited resources is that much of its income was contributed to the church, a major component of Tongan communal life.

Masa described his family as caring. "When I was getting into trouble and fights my mother was always protecting me and my father would snap. Many of their arguments were about me. They loudly expressed their disappointment in me. Very loudly."

Masa, like many young kids, dreamed of becoming a star athlete when he grew up. "My goal when I was about elementary age was to play football. I also trained for about two years in boxing. My biggest disappointment in high school was that I never had the opportunity to play football. With all the motivation it might be hard to understand why I couldn't stay in school, but I couldn't get out of the lifestyle. I had enemies and a reputation. I was too far in. There were days I wanted to quit, but I didn't know how. I went to a high school in the good part of town during my freshman year and thought I could get a fresh start, but immediately I ran into three brothers from KPT (a public housing project in Kalihi) and we got into it. I broke one of my hands. I lasted at Kalani High School for all of five days. We were all arrested and they got suspended. I returned to Farrington and got kicked out again. I went to a couple of other schools and it was the same story. Pretty soon everybody was frustrated with me.

"My parents loved me but didn't know what to do with me so they sent me to live with my auntie in San Bernardino. I lived with her for two months and got into plenty of trouble over there. California was just another weird place for me. No matter what, I always found where the action was at and always happened to get involved. I had traded one ghetto for another and found my way into gangs through my cousins." He later wrote in a college English paper, "Kalihifornia [combining Kalihi and California] was the place where the killers are from, so I had to change my whole lifestyle so I could be one of them killaz or be eaten alive."

After two months in San Bernardino, he was shipped off to another relative in Englewood in the notorious South Central Los Angeles community, where he quickly adopted its violent gang lifestyle. His family was afraid that if he stayed he would get killed, so they sent him back to Hawaii. He was only gone from Hawaii for four months.

His problems only became worse upon his return. The Family now became his whole life. The gang adopted the motto, "No guts, no glory." He said, "We lived by it, honored it, cherished it, and would die for it. We didn't care what others thought. We were beyond a gang, we were family. We were united in every way."

He began to understand, however, that notoriety came with a price. He wrote, "Life was getting harder and harder each day. I was Oahu's most wanted. Everyone wanted a piece of me. Everywhere I went someone would be challenging me because of my reputation. I was shot at, banged, stabbed, mobbed, and baseball-batted, but each time I got them back. I never forgot their faces and what they did to me."

Masa's recall of his life, written several years after the events occurred, is vivid. "One day a lot of us cut classes and went to the house of one of the boys. Shortly after school was out a friend of ours was shot at school. It started a war and the chain reaction that at the time seemed like it would never end. I remember being so pissed off that I was ready to kill. The other gangs were lucky because the cops came down on us like a ton of bricks. Sometimes I wish I had been the one who was shot because my friend was so innocent and harmless. The thing escalated. Now we weren't only rivals with other gangs, the cops were also getting involved. Every day we would get searched, and then they would beat us. There was no sense filing a complaint because we were gang members. Whenever there was trouble I would be the first guy arrested even if I wasn't there.

"We were getting tired of the police brutality, and tired of being ignored when we complained about being attacked by other gangs. When we did complain or tried to file charges the cops told us to handle it ourselves. On the other hand if complaints were filed against us we were quickly arrested. So we took the advice of the cops and decided to handle things our way.

"Some of us got together and made Molotov cocktails and took them to a dance. We knew our enemies would be there. They started eyeing us up as soon as we arrived. When they began to get aggressive we knew we couldn't handle them because we were so far outnumbered, so we ran outside. Two guys lit their homemade bombs and threw them, and everybody ran back inside. Then I saw the cop that I hated the most coming down on us. I hated him because every time he saw me he beat me. I climbed a wall and lit my gas bomb. His car door was open so I let my bomb go. He closed the door and escaped with his car on fire. I watched him and felt all the hate in the world flow through me. The only emotion I felt was pure hate.

"A couple of weeks later I found myself up against the Bloods. I had been fighting with them since third grade. When they jumped me I pulled my knife and got their leader. My first stab went through his stomach. When he hit the ground I went for his heart, but his hand got in the way, so it went through his hand and stuck over an inch into his chest. I took it out and stuck him again in the shoulder. I took off after hearing police sirens, but before I did, I spit in his face. I felt no pity and no regret. All I felt was relief because I knew he would never bother me again.

"I was soon arrested and charged with second-degree attempted murder. I was only fourteen years old but had already been arrested about thirty-eight times. Two times for attempted murder. I had eleven pending cases, including assault on a police officer. My number was finally up, but a deal was arranged with immigration to temporarily deport me to Tonga. I didn't want to go but as things stood I had little choice.

"When I got there it was straight to boarding school. My first year I was captain of my class. I tried band and played rugby. At first I wasn't very good at rugby, because I had never played it before and was teased by relatives who were very good players. They compared me to my father who had been well-known in the sport. They even showed me old newspaper articles at the library about him."

The teasing that Masa experienced motivated him. His goal was to be as good, and perhaps even better, than his father, and also to shut up his critics. By his senior year he had made a name for himself in the sport and was picked for the Tonga National Team (under-nineteen) and had the opportunity to represent Tonga in a tournament played in New Zealand and Fiji. The team won five out of seven games. Even though it didn't win the tournament, Masa said, "I was so happy because it was the first time I reached a goal that I had made. I felt so good because I had realized a dream that I couldn't accomplish in Hawaii. All my life I wanted to play football, but never had the chance because of all the trouble that I got into."

Masa's four-year life in Tonga gave him insight on what his abilities were. It was a totally different experience from Hawaii and California. In addition to rugby he was in the school band (he still plays guitar), choir director, and honor-roll student. He felt trusted and respected. He said his parents were, "totally blown away because they thought I had no talent besides fighting and breaking the law."

In addition to his successful school experience he learned how to survive off of the land with very little money. He learned to grow things and cook, and he found that he liked it.

Religion also found him. He said, "Learning how to pray was thrilling and exciting. The most horrifying experience that I ever faced was when I had to pray in front of 1,500 students. But I managed to survive, and when it was over I felt like a large weight was lifted off of my shoulders. It was the best feeling I ever had in my entire life. It's very difficult to explain."

Masa had mixed feelings about the Tongan period of his life. Although it was a time of success and relative peace, it was also a far more primitive environment than what was familiar to him. He recalled, "When I finally graduated from there, I was feeling all good because I could say that I'd earned my diploma, 'cause I had to put up with hell and go through hell to save myself." On the other hand, when he was offered a scholarship to return to attend college and play his last year of rugby, he said, "I was happy and willing to go back because I had gotten used to the lifestyle and enjoyed it." The decision to stay in Tonga or to leave was also debated by his mother and father. His mother was all for having him remain, but his father wanted him to return to Hawaii, and his wishes prevailed. Masa himself had doubts about returning, but hoped that he could bury his past. He wanted to believe that after four years away people would have forgotten about him. "Damn, was I wrong. My past was still being talked about like it was yesterday. No matter what I tried it was always there. Slowly my dream of a new life began to fade away… just like a dream."

When Masa returned to Hawaii he was dismayed to find that his old neighborhood had been taken over by drug dealers and the "druggies" who were their customers. Traffic in and out of the park was persistent, yet the police did little to challenge it. He was shocked that sales were taking place in front of the little kids who played there, and was determined to do something to stop it. He pulled his friends together and put an end to the problem. Unfortunately, there were those in the neighborhood, because of the group's history, who saw them not as the solution but as the problem.

When Masa was nineteen his life finally seemed to be on track. He was attending community college and working as a dispatcher for a baggage transfer company at the airport. One morning he received an excited call from a co-worker who wanted him to bring a gun to the office because he had heard they were going to get robbed. Masa said, "Without thinking I just took a gun down there." That evening a drive-by occurred at the park. "I was relieved to find out that I didn't know the boy who had gotten shot, but I went to pick up many of my friends who might be around there. After I dropped them off at home, I pulled into the gas station by my friend's house and was confronted by members of a rival gang. One of the guys got a gun from one of his friends and started to walk toward me pointing the gun at my head. I stepped on the gas and the engine just revved. I forgot I was in neutral. I leaned over toward the passenger seat. I thought I was going to die, but as I was leaning over I felt the gun in my waist band. I had forgotten about it. I pulled it out and pointed it at him. I was thinking 'if I die, he's coming with me.' He and I had a brief standoff and then he ran. My heart was pounding and I just wanted to get out of there. I put the gun on the passenger's seat and took off. When I hit the main street I looked over and saw the guy with the gun tracking me. I heard a pop. I don't remember seeing a flash because I was on the wrong side of the road and car lights were coming toward me. Reflexively, I searched for my gun and shot back. I didn't know what to do. I was confused and in shock, so I drove to the airport and told my co-worker what had happened. It wasn't long before the Crime Reduction Unit cops showed up. The night was turning into a nightmare. Everything had happened so fast. It was like a bad dream."

A member of the rival gang, but not the boy with the gun, was shot in the lower leg, apparently from a ricochet. Masa was charged with attempted murder in the first degree, two counts of attempted murder in the second degree, three counts of terroristic threatening, and one count of place to keep a firearm. Bail was set at $335,000. His trial was held nine months later. All this time he was incarcerated at the Oahu Community Correctional Center. At trial he was acquitted of all charges except, "place to keep a firearm," and released from prison a few days later. He was sentenced, subsequently, to six months of prison and five years' probation, with credit for time served.

After his release he appeared disoriented for several weeks. The twinkle in his eyes was gone and he was uncomfortable around people. With the help of his family and friends he slowly began to heal. After a time he met with the boy who was shot, and they agreed, in everybody's best interest, to put the past behind them. It was a bold move, and sent a signal to both of their groups to finally end their ten-year rivalry. No one could remember how it got started in the first place.

Masa demonstrated enormous resiliency. A few weeks after his sentencing, with support from Adult Friends for Youth and a grant from the City and County of Honolulu, he and a group of his friends began their own T-shirt design business. They learned silk-screening, purchasing, production, selling, and money management. He assumed a leadership role and, in a letter to the *Honolulu Advertiser*, he wrote, "Original Graphics is something we can call our own. It's something we can wake up feeling good about. I wish there were opportunities for other youths. I wish they could also go from being destructive to constructive people like we have. There is no future for us or anyone else in maintaining the dangerous lifestyle; I know, I've been part of it at its worst."

Who he was and what he wanted to become changed as he grew older. In Tonga he thought about becoming an accountant so that he wouldn't have to deal with people and in fact enrolled in a community college business administration course when he returned to Hawaii. He reflected that in the beginning he liked the fights and the gang life. He had a lot of confidence and always won his fights, but as he grew older he said, "I became tired, I couldn't get out of the lifestyle. I had enemies and a reputation. I was in too deep. I never became afraid, but life had no meaning. I got to the point where I didn't care whether I lived or died, and sometimes I just wanted to die. I suppose that made me a pretty dangerous person."

When asked if he thought about suicide, he replied, "Many times. Once I tried to shoot myself, but the gun wouldn't go off. I had hit rock bottom. I was on drugs. Everything was falling apart. My only income was from robbing. I couldn't get a job. Even McDonald's wouldn't hire me. They're supposed to hire everybody, right? I tried all kinds of places. My friends got jobs, but no one would hire me. Maybe it was the way I looked. I couldn't even get an interview. At the time I tried to shoot myself I put the gun to my head, and pulled the trigger but nothing happened. When I looked at the bullet it had a firing pin mark. I pointed the gun out the window and shot up all the blinds. My girlfriend was in the room and my parents were in the house. They tried to break down the door. I put the gun in my mouth and again it wouldn't fire. I was just tired. It was time to go." When asked why he didn't try again, he replied, "I ran out of bullets. I pointed it at her, and was planning to shoot her too. We just cried afterwards."

A week later Masa was arrested for probation violation and went back to prison. He was twenty-two years old at the time. A number of painful events, beginning with the shooting of the rival gang member when he was nineteen, preceded these dark days.

Masa was attending community college. Not only was he a good student, but he was well-liked and respected by his instructors. One morning, as he was at home getting ready to go to school, the Immigration and Naturalization Service came and got him. The possession of a firearm conviction that seemed minor at the time was anything but a small thing to the federal government. The U.S. Attorney General saw it as a "high crime." The process of "removal" (deportation) began. He was sent to the San Pedro Federal Correction Center at Terminal Island, California, to be processed. He described his feelings as being, "angry, very angry." Just as his life was on track and he felt he was finally moving forward everything came crashing down. Within days he was whisked away, never expecting to return to Hawaii. It was September 1996, just four months after his sentencing and release from prison.

Adult Friends for Youth was anguished that the young man who had worked so hard to turn his life around was about to be forcibly stripped from his family and friends just as he was seeing the light at the end of a very dark tunnel. The agency was able to locate an attorney who was willing to visit Masa at Terminal Island before returning to Hawaii from Washington, DC. He gave Masa hope and provided advice on securing his release. Masa subsequently was able to secure a bail hearing. A sympathetic judge set bail at $2,000 and Masa was released and returned to Hawaii. Subsequent court hearings resulted in indefinite postponement of further deportation proceedings.

In January 1997 he returned to college. Life again was getting back on track. That September, despite all that he had experienced, nothing was like the devastation that would consume him when his beloved younger sister, with whom he was very close, died suddenly from a heart attack as she was dressing for school. There was no preparation for this tragedy. He said that he could deal with his own death, but didn't know how to deal with her dying. He descended into depression, and spent much time at her grave site. Feelings of hopelessness, despair, and suicide became constant companions. He was consumed by guilt and blamed himself for his sister's death, believing that she was made to pay for his misdeeds. In spite of his pain he returned to college but found it difficult to concentrate. Although light occasionally found his dark corners, it wasn't enough. A year later he made the attempt to end his life.

Adult Friends for Youth has been a constant in Masa's life for twenty years, from the time he was thirteen to the present. Despite all that life has thrown at him he has persevered. He eventually earned a Master of Social Work degree, and was the commencement speaker for his class. He distinguished himself academically and has set a high bar in clinical practice, working with young people who mirror the violent young man he was. In our first book, we hypothesized that a former gang member who has earned academic credentials can be a strong asset to a therapeutic gang-intervention program. Masa is evidence that the hypothesis has merit.

Masa concluded the interview by describing his relationship with AFY, as a client.

"Before I met Debbie (Deborah Spencer-Chun) everybody labeled me as a violent person. But when I met her she wasn't afraid of me. She didn't judge me as a bad kid. She saw the best in me. She always told us 'I love you. I worry about you.' I never heard from my parents that they loved me. It's a cultural thing. To tell a boy that you love him is to make him weak. A bad memory for me is that once, when

I was in the hospital, after being beaten with a baseball bat in a gang fight, and was out of it, my father showed me no sympathy. He only wanted to know what I did wrong.

"People didn't believe that I could change, but Debbie was always there, encouraging me like, 'You can do it, you can do it. You can go to college.' I never thought I had the ability to do anything.

"She was always there, twenty-four-seven. We'd call her at three o'clock in the morning—'Debbie, we just got into a fight in Waipahu and we're stranded.' She would pick us up without complaining and would talk to us. She would ask what happened, but never in a tone where we felt she was blaming us.

"AFY didn't come in giving the impression that they know what's best. They let us make decisions. Adults think they know what is best, but ultimately kids will make their own decisions. Kids know what they want but don't know how to get it. AFY provided the 'how' by helping us explore options. We talked things through, and then we decided. When we made decisions, we took responsibility. It helped us build confidence in ourselves.

"The turning point for me, after going through a lot of personal pain, was when Deb and Sid got a scholarship for me in 2001. At first I thought that if I did this I'd get them off my back. They had more confidence in me than I had in me. My first semester I had one A, two Bs, and a C. I never had an A before, and I thought, 'Wow an A,' but then I looked at the C and thought, that's not so good. It was a good thing that AFY has a no termination policy, because I was always able to go back whenever I was feeling down.

"Through Debbie I began to get in touch with my feelings. When I was with the boys everything shut down. You can't feel on the streets. Feelings get you killed. You just have to react. I've always had two hearts, but I had to camouflage it. My roles had to change with different people."

The chameleon in him was reflected in a public presentation he made on what it was like to be a gang member. He recalled, "I had a friend in a rival gang, and we would sneak around and drink and do things together, but if our groups fought we would go against each other, and later we would get together and see if we were okay."

Masa said that he felt that Debbie was someone who he could always trust. "When she said, 'I'll be there for you guys,' she meant it. Other people, from the time I was small, said that, but when it came time to prove it nobody was home. She gave us hope. For many of us there was no hope. When you get into the lifestyle, hope begins to disappear. You get to the point where you don't care whether you live or die and so why should you care whether anyone else lives or dies is the way you begin to think.

"When I was ready to commit suicide I didn't call Debbie because I had pride. That's one of my issues, I have too much pride. One thing, I was on drugs and I didn't want her to see me. The thing that most of us in the gang lacked was self-confidence. Debbie and AFY helped us to build that. When we started the T-shirt business we were able to come out into the real world and feel that we could make it. When I was at the point of deepest despair and I wanted to kill myself I felt I couldn't ask any more of Deb. I had taken enough." All my life I felt I had taken from other people, and never given back. (Until this interview was conducted Deb never knew how close Masa had come to killing himself.)

The role that AFY played in helping dropout and push-out members of the group to attend and graduate from alternative schools helped many of them turn away from gang-banging (AFY established its own alternative school in 2001). The agency also exposed Masa and his friends to new experiences. He recalled that the first time the group made a trip to the University of Hawaii campus he went with a chip on his shoulder, and actually called out one of the students who was smaller than him. He was embarrassed at the memory. Nevertheless, it was his first introduction to the institution from which he would later receive both bachelor's and master's degrees.

Masa said the group respected Debbie, "Just the way she carried herself. She wasn't afraid of us. She would tell us straight what she thought. Other people would beat around the bush—kiss our butts.

Most of my life I felt like I was walking around in the dark. Daylight came once a week for two hours when we had our group sessions. I was limited in what I could do and where I could go because of my reputation, but AFY gave me an opportunity to do fun things, like bowling, pool, and going to the beach, without having to watch my back."

Deb's relationship with the boys went much further than the group's weekly sessions. There were also a lot of individual counseling sessions, and her individual work with Masa went on for years. As close as the boys were to each other and as much as they could discuss issues in the group there were certain personal issues that, if exposed, would in their eyes make them vulnerable and cause cracks in their reputations. Masa explained, "I wouldn't share too much about my feelings in the group because if you showed blood the sharks might come in and eat you, but I always felt comfortable to talk about personal things with Debbie."

Twenty years have passed since AFY's first encounter with Masa's group. He said most of the boys are doing well now. They didn't go on to become gangsters. He credits AFY for this positive outcome, and noted, "People who didn't know what our gang was all about wouldn't understand. We took on everybody. We were hard core, and willing to kill for each other. But, one by one, we began to change. All the years and tears finally paid off. Now when we get together we can laugh about the past. We're lucky. We are all lucky. The gang-banging mentality is a thing of the past. When the men come together now a lot of times it's family stuff. We bring the kids along. The friendships remain. They worry about their kids getting into gangs and drugs.

"Now that I am a social worker I better understand how I was helped and what my clients are experiencing. I can appreciate the stress they are under. I know how to deal with stress. I've had to deal with it my whole life.

"My past reputation has not caused me any problems in my social-work practice, except sometimes with the cops. When I go into the projects my former enemies accept the work that I do with kids and they encourage me to help. They know that I'm sincere.

"AFY has been unique in helping kids get in touch with their emotions. I was one of those that had a hard time with my emotions. I experienced life in one ghetto in Hawaii and other ghettos on the mainland. The issues for youth are the same. Redirectional Therapy works in Hawaii and would also work on the mainland. If we start with the young boys, the OGs (original gangsters) won't interfere, and might encourage it. They get tired, too."

Francisco

This was the only interview conducted outside of Hawaii. It took place at the Gold Coast Hotel in Las Vegas in March 2009, following lunch that included four AFY staff members, Francisco, his wife, and their two small daughters. Francisco was one of the more notorious gang-bangers of The Babies, a group AFY worked with in the late 1980s and through the early 1990s. He is now in his middle thirties.

We took advantage of this opportunity to catch up with him during a ten-day mainland trip that included presentations on AFY and Redirectional Therapy in California, Nevada, Utah, and Washington. He had moved several years earlier. His children were born in Las Vegas where he is a successful master auto mechanic.

This is what Francisco had to say.

"I came from the Philippines when I was five years old with my mom, a brother who is two years younger than me, and an older brother and sister. My father was already here and working. I never had support like I give my kids now. I have often thought that if I had a different family my life would have turned out a lot better."

Francisco came from a broken home. By the time he was ten years old his father was living with a girlfriend. He said, "I asked my mother why he didn't come home at night and she would make excuses like, 'He's at work.' My parents weren't educated so I wasn't influenced in that direction. I tried to explain to my younger sister when she would get angry with my mother that without an education she was doing her best, and it was especially difficult for her because most of the time my father wasn't around. I respected my mother because she was present when my father was absent. My father was a baker and had most of the money.

"Nobody ever read to us when we were children. I missed all that. I try now to be a much better parent to my two girls. I am always there for them."

Francisco's mother worked from time to time, but, because his older brother has Down syndrome he took up much of her time.

"There was a lot of frustration at home because of all the effort that went into taking care of him. It was tough on my mother raising four kids, including one with special needs."

The chaotic nature of the apartment in which the family lived appears to have been a factor that pushed Francisco and his younger brother into the gang life. Among the problems in the house was the ongoing fighting between father and mother. He said that he tried to help out financially by selling newspapers and earning money for himself so that he wouldn't be a burden. He acknowledged that he was very angry.

In the apartment building there were other boys with whom he hung out. They had older relatives that were members of a notorious gang that was prominent in the eighties. They took on their name and became the Babies. By the time Francisco was thirteen he began to identify himself as a gang member. He said, "At the beginning we mostly were doing graffiti and being public nuisances like making loud noises and pushing our weight around. Then the fighting and violence grew. We even initiated each other. It sounds crazy now but even though we were the original members we beat each other up. The idea was that if we were going to initiate new members we should initiate ourselves to be fair. The reason for an initiation at all was to find out how much a member could take. The original group included me, and my brother, who was sixteen. Later as we grew we had factions all over the place including Waipahu, Salt Lake, Moanalua, Kalihi, and McKinley High School. Sometimes there were big meetings when all the groups would come together. The groups had officers, like president and vice president. The OGs influenced the younger boys and meetings were often called by them."

Francisco became one of the leaders, and his younger brother, Roberto, played a key role in initiating new members. Initiations were actually pretty simple, but violent. A new member was blindfolded and one member just pounded on him.

When asked what the group meant to him, Francisco replied, "If I got into trouble somebody was there to help me out. I was the first guy to get involved when somebody made trouble to us. I used to fight a lot. I guess I got into that spot because I had so much anger in me. When I went home there was never anyone there for me. Violence was the way to express my anger." When asked if he ever felt suicidal, he replied, "I didn't feel that way because I was more into fighting. I didn't want to kill the other guy. I just wanted to hurt him."

Francisco's life changed when he was sixteen. A fight had broken out at Kalakaua Intermediate School involving a friend. He was running to help him out. A security guard saw him, grabbed him from the back, and threw him to the ground.

Francisco described what happened next. "The guard was a big guy and he just picked me up and body-slammed me to the ground. When I was on the ground he kneed me in the stomach. He was way over two-hundred fifty pounds and I was just one-hundred thirty at the time. He landed on my stomach full force. I yelled, but he stayed on me for some time. I was in a lot of pain. After he let me up I tried to walk a little but I collapsed. I finally got up and walked home. I tried to sleep, but after a half hour I got up and started to throw up blood. I told my mother and she and a neighbor took me to the doctor and he told us to go to the emergency room.

"I had two surgeries. The majority of my pancreas was removed. There was a financial settlement with the state, but it wasn't enough. We were pretty naïve and got taken advantage of. They paid the medical bills, but there was very little for pain and suffering. I wish we could go back and do it all over again. What worked against me, I think, was that I had a reputation as a bad boy. Twenty years later, I am on a diet and have to watch what I eat."

The security guard never testified at the hearing. Francisco later learned that he suffered a stroke and died.

After the injury, Francisco's leadership role in the gang declined and he began to loosen his ties with it. He gave up his bad behavior and it wasn't long before the group began to break up.

He now sees what happened to him as a "blessing in disguise." "If it hadn't happened I would be dead or in prison. It was a life-changing experience in many ways."

When asked what role AFY played in changing his life and the lives of the other gang members he replied, "AFY was always there for us. It was like being part of a family. Somebody we could talk to and that kept us out of trouble. Deb had a heart for us. She communicated with us and we opened up to her. We could always count on her. We knew that she would be there for us every Friday or whenever we needed her. If it wasn't for her we would all be different." Francisco never graduated from high school but his brother did. However, he did go on to attend and graduate from a trade school where he majored in auto mechanics and fulfilled the occupational goal that he had had from the time he was in intermediate school. It troubles him that he doesn't have a high school diploma. He said that he hopes to one day go back and get it. He commented, "I know people who have a diploma but no education. I'm just the opposite. I have an education but no diploma. Sometimes I feel a little guilty that I've become successful and make a good living without it."

He emphasized that his relationship with AFY was like a close family relationship. He said, "Like now, when you came to Las Vegas, we got together. Even though I hadn't talked with Debbie for years, when I talked with her a couple of days ago it was like talking to an old friend. AFY was like family when we had no family to help us. This was especially important to my brother, who is also doing good today. The things I need to concentrate on in the future are my health and to see my girls graduate.

"If I ever make good money I would like to donate it to you guys because you help a lot of people."

At the end of the interview, while expressing his strong feelings for the help he and his friends had received from AFY, he became quite emotional and his eyes filled with tears. He truly believes in AFY's potential to help young people. He also believes, because of the person he has become, that his girls will go to college and will have the life that he never had.

Jose

Jose was born in the Philippines in 1987 and came to Hawaii when he was nine years old. He had attended a private Catholic school and had learned enough English to understand it, but had difficulty speaking it when he first arrived. He described his life in the Philippines as middle class and economically stable. He said, "There was always enough to eat. We didn't have to struggle to survive. I never felt poor."

His grandfather's brother on his father's side was the first member of the family to emigrate to Hawaii to work in the sugar cane fields. He brought Jose's grandfather, who in turn brought his children. On his mother's side only his mother emigrated, at the insistence of her husband.

Jose has three brothers and a sister, but there was an older brother that he never knew and about whom his parents never spoke. He died of an undisclosed illness at age fourteen on the same day that Jose was born. He didn't become aware of his brother's existence until he was fifteen, when it was revealed in a casual conversation that he had with an uncle.

When Jose first arrived in Hawaii he thought it was great. His extended family was welcoming and lived well. He observed that even the air felt better. "Hawaii was amazing," he recalled. "My family and the people I met before I started school were all friendly, but once I started school it was a different story. I felt really out of place. I was so quiet. At recess all the other kids were running around. I remember just being alone. After a time some of my classmates came up and talked to me."

Jose became aware of gangs when he was in fifth or sixth grade, mostly through older students. He said that kids hung out in cliques, but they weren't gangs. He noted that the difference was that cliques were just groups of friends. "The clique became a gang when someone did something wrong and others backed him up. When that happened the group was perceived as a gang. It was a matter of perception."

Q. It seems that there is an evolution. The group starts out as a clique. Then somebody gets into a fight with someone from another clique and the group backs him up and then it kind of escalates.

A. Yep. That's the way I remember it. The first time I thought of gangs was when I was in seventh grade. Then I began to see the violence between different races involving the Samoans. Different races cruised with their own. Filipinos with Filipinos, Hawaiians with Hawaiians, Samoans with Samoans. Like that. That's just the way it was back then. I didn't want to get into fights but I had to, especially when older friends in the eighth grade were involved. It was very common in intermediate school. I was actually afraid. There was a time when we fought every lunchtime. The Samoans had a group called WUTANG (Waipahu United Thugs And Notorious Gangsters). It was a coalition of Samoans and locals against Filipinos.

In the middle of the seventh grade Jose was recruited by the MM gang. The initials stood for *Matirang Matibuy*—Only the Strong Survive. This was a clean break from the clique he had known before. It introduced him into the heavy gang life. From "seeing his friends getting beaten up by the Samoan guys," he was drawn into the MM from fear that he would suffer the same fate unless he had protection.

Q. What would have happened had you not joined?

A. That's a question that I've always asked myself, because when eighth grade came I was just more confident in myself. I became a leader in our group after the eighth-graders moved up to high school. I had several fights back then for stupid reasons. It was ironic because I was friends with a lot of Samoans too.

Q. These gangs were not neighbor groups. They originated at school?

A. Yes. I didn't actually become a member of MM until high school. In the eighth grade I got into lots of fights with Hawaiians, Samoans, and local guys. Fights were usually one-on-one but sometimes I got mobbed. It was crazy. They saw me as the leader of my group. I was the tallest and biggest one. Even though I tried to deny that I was a gang member that was the way I was seen by others. Although my group didn't have a name I was singled out as the leader of my clique.

Q. Is that why MM recruited you?

A. I don't know, but there was one moment that I remember. I was with my friend Michael in a car. He was in the gang and he was telling me all about the recruiting. He said you don't have to join, you can just cruise with us, but I decided to join. I don't know why. One day they led ten of us to this place by a pond where they hung out and the initiation began. They blindfolded us with their yellow rags and told us to stand on this log. The next thing I knew I heard bottles being smashed against the log and they told us to jump off this log—it was maybe six inches high—onto a mat with the broken glass in our bare feet.

Q. Didn't you get cut?

A. It was small cuts.

Q. Didn't it bleed?

A. A little, but not bad. After we jumped we could take the rags off, but then we had to put them back on and they beat us with their boards. They lined us up at the edge of the pond and told us to put our hands up over our heads and scream 'MM.' It was crazy.

Q. How did you feel going through it?

A. I felt I was ready for this. I was just going to take it on. All the older guys took a whack and there were a lot of them. When I was finished I saw the other guys and their legs was trembling.

Q. How badly hurt were you from all of this?

A. I just had a bruise on the back of my thigh.

Q. Were they swinging to hurt you?

A. Yes. That's how it is in the Philippines. They do it like that.

After the initiation, meetings were held once a week that involved training where we would fight each other. Part of the initiation involved a formal swearing-in where the new members swore loyalty to the gang.

Q. After you were sworn in what did your role in the group become?

A. In my freshman year, I was first a soldier, I guess. I was following the older guys. When they left—some graduated, some were sent to other schools, and some were kicked out—I became second-in-command, and eventually the leader of the in-school group. There was still an older group that was out of school. They sometimes gave us orders, but I didn't see them that much. There were like two people in me. When I was introduced to this life I was a good student. I did all of my work. I was a good person school-wise, but when I became part of that it became difficult to manage both. It caught up to me. I began to do things that weren't the right things for me. Part of me wanted to do the right things and excel in school and the other part felt a loyalty and commitment to the gang.

Q. So how did it work out?

A. I guess the gang-banger won out. I met a lot of people in school. Most of them respected me. I played sports.

Q. What was it like at Waipahu High School? Were there a lot of groups?

A. Yeah, a lot.

The second semester of sophomore year I got kicked out because I got caught with a joint on me. A security guard saw me. I got kicked out for a semester. I went to an alternative school—Hale O'ulu. It was cool. No gangs. Just guys who had screwed up (Jose actually graduated with his Waipahu Class).

Q. What were your parents going through at this time?

A. They didn't know I was in a gang.

Q. How about when you got kicked out of school?

A. They were pissed, but they still accepted me.

Q. How would you describe your parents?

A. They're good parents. They talked to me. When I was a kid they laid their hands on me but as I got older they talked to me. They were understanding.

Q. Who was the disciplinarian in the family?

A. My father. I never felt abused. He was fair. He disciplined me when I deserved it.

Q. What makes a gang a gang?

A. Building power. To see who is the strongest and who is in control. It's all about power. Who's stronger than who. Power comes through violence, gang-banging.

Q. Besides the gang-banging what other criminal or destructive behaviors did the gang get into?

A. Drugs, alcohol. We did all of that—ice, weed—even as young kids. Sometimes we looked for trouble and sometimes it came to us.

Q. Did you ever fear for your life?

A. Yes, I was afraid, but you had the other members with you so you felt secure and no matter what happens you have to be strong. Sometimes we would chase other gangs in cars, like high-speed chases. It was like we would know where they would be like at a party, and we would go mess it up not even knowing whose party it was, but just that our rivals were there, mostly it was other Filipino gangs. When Michael got stabbed it escalated into this big thing. Anything could get it started. Somebody giving you the eye, or a rival gang member talking to someone's girlfriend. Girls are often part of the problem. In Michael's situation it was over a girl. Michael's anger was unreal. They had been together a long time. That's what started all the fire, and we got carried along with it, and he got stabbed too.

Q. How would you describe your childhood and adolescence?

A. (Long pause) I was always fighting two people in me. There were always voices in my head telling me I got to do this or that. I get angry. I get happy.

Q. How would you describe your feelings most of the time?

A. Confused. Overwhelmed.

Q. Can you describe the best time growing up and also the worst time?

A. The best times were getting together with all the relatives. When we had parties and everybody was there. The worst time was when your parents got dysfunctional, the way they talk to each other when they talk about things financially, like what kinds of things to pay for. They don't realize that it affects us.

Q. You say dysfunctional. Do you mean when your parents fight?

A. Yeah, they used to constantly fight. They fought both verbally and physically. It was really upsetting. They fought in the Philippines, too. I have constant flashbacks to it when I was a child. I trip out—how could I remember that, but I do. I can't understand how I remember that. I was only about five or six, but I remember all of those things.

Q. Do you believe that life was any different for you than for your friends?

A. I believe it was pretty similar. Everybody has a battle. It's just in a different sense. My parents are still together, but they always talk about divorce. My father has a hard time talking about how he feels, but he said she just wants to go. My mother said that he wants to go back to the Philippines. He wants to leave us. She told me she told him to just go and leave us.

Jose's mother works as a hotel housekeeper. His father works most of the time as a security guard. It has been more difficult for his father economically in Hawaii than in the Philippines. His mother came to Hawaii reluctantly. She came because her husband wanted to come to join his family. None of her family lives in Hawaii. Both mother and father return to the Philippines periodically for visits.

Q. What were the best and worst things about being in the gang?

A. The adrenaline rushes. Never thinking about the dangers or consequences. Crashing parties of rivals. The power. You want other people to know who you are. The worst time was when I was jumped by my own gang. Before it happened the vibes weren't right at the party. When the party broke up and we were moving toward our cars, bam, it just happened. I was so confused by what was happening. I didn't even know

> what I was feeling. What happened before I was jumped was that I called another member's girlfriend to find out where everybody was and got into a conversation with her, just as a friend. She took it as I was coming on to her, and she told the others and it just escalated from there, and the group decided to punish me. Up to that time I believed they were all my friends. The girl's boyfriend wasn't there at the time of the beating. He came right after. The leader of the gang was the most aggressive and caused a wound that left a permanent scar. To this day I don't speak to them. When I was walking away I was screaming at them, 'the f--- is this?' From that day on I had had no relationship with them. It was the end of my gang life.

Some boys that Jose knew from when he first moved to Hawaii were at the party, but they weren't part of the gang and weren't involved. He remains friends with them. He said that during the beating, when he was on the ground, he went for his knife and jumped up and went for them, especially the girl's boyfriend who had showed up. "It was the girl's fault too," he said. "That night was awkward. I had gotten off work and went home to change and took the bus to the party. It was eight-thirty to nine o'clock so I took my knife. When I was on the bus I thought, 'why do I have my knife, I'm going to a party with friends.'"

Q. You mentioned your knife. Were weapons part of the gang life?
A. Yes, but it isn't like the mainland where they have guns. But knives and pellet guns, and bats, yes.
Q. Did you usually have a knife on you at school?
A. Most of the time, but I didn't need it.
Q. Was it common for others to pack weapons?
A. Yeah.
Q. You played football? What was the experience like?
A. Only in my senior year. I wish I had played all four years. I played basketball all my four years.
Q. Did your parents ever come to your games?

A. No. My father never did.

Q. Would you have wanted him to see you play?

A. Of course. One time two of my brothers and my mother came. That was the only time. I brought home lots of trophies.

Q. Did your mother or father ever say they were proud of you?

A. Nope. They never said that.

Q. Did they ever say they loved you?

A. (He laughed). No.

Q. Did you ever want them to?

A. I never expected them to.

Q. If you ever have children of your own?

A. Of course. That's what I've learned. But I don't blame them or anything. But I'm going to do my best to be a better person.

Q. When did AFY come into your life?

A. My freshman year. My brother used to be a client. He had a white shirt with a rainbow on the back and I asked him, 'What's that?' Some of my friends were involved and they brought me in.

Q. How do you feel AFY and Debbie impacted your life?

A. There was also Mo and Udella. It was Debbie and Mo most of the time. Sometimes even Mac and Misi.

Q. Did they help you feel better about yourself?

A. Something like Debbie reaching out and shaking my hand was like I felt respected. Other adults don't do that. They are adults but they also make you feel that they are friends. With the gang I would always call Debbie or Mo. The night I was attacked by my gang I called Debbie, and Debbie and Mo came to the hospital. They were always available to talk to. I miss those days of being their client. It gave me comfort knowing that they were there. I looked forward to having group every week. I looked forward to the outings and the therapy stuff they did with us talking about our issues.

Q. Where are you with your life now?

A. Honestly, I don't have a clear plan of what I want to do.

Jose has changed his mind many times about what he wants to do. He had plans to attend a prestigious aeronautical university and talked about becoming a pilot. He even took flying lessons. He also expressed an interest in becoming an electrician.

Q. Do you still see some of your old friends?

A. Just my homeboys, the people I grew up with, but not from the gang. The gang-banging is over already. My friends now have families, are going to school or working. Growing up is a hard thing to do. I am overwhelmed by it. My dad wants me to go into the military. Half of me wants to do it, but the other half doesn't.

Q. Did you ever think about suicide to the point where you began to plan it out?

A. I thought about it, but not where I planned it out. I thought about it lots of times. I've had dreams about it, like shooting myself. I've thought about how the world would be different if I wasn't in it. Sometimes I feel so confused.

Jose attended community college for two years but never received an AA. He acknowledges that one of his biggest problems is self-discipline.

Recently Jose's plan to become an electrician began to develop. AFY's relationship with the local chapter of the International Brotherhood of Electrical Workers (IBEW) led to lengthy interviews and testing. Both Jose and another AFY client passed the national exam and were offered scholarships. Their apprenticeship began in March 2011.

Rolando

Rolando, at age thirty-four, is a solid citizen. He is a journeyman in a skilled trade. He has a good job with an excellent salary, is married, has his own home, runs a foster care center for older adults with his wife, and is involved in civic affairs. He is an active member of his community and well respected in his trade. His tales of his earlier life, however, are chilling.

He moved to Hawaii from the Philippines when he was twelve years old. School was a scary place for him. He was placed in a special class for non-English-speaking students and was picked on every day. He said he was called all kinds of names like, "fresh off the boat" and "buk buk," a derogatory term for immigrant Filipinos. He recalled that one time someone spit in his face. "So the only thing I could do to get accepted was to join a gang," he said.

Q. Were those that treated you so badly gang members?

A. Yes, they were.

Q. The gang that you joined was The Family. What drew you to them?

A. The Family were guys like me. They came from the Philippines. We spoke the same language. I joined them because another immigrant, who was a friend of mine, joined. I joined a year after I arrived. I was in the eighth grade. It was hard being an immigrant. I felt embarrassed. I felt alone. I couldn't speak what was on my mind. It was frustrating. It just wasn't comfortable. I didn't want to go to school. The Family made me feel comfortable. It felt like a brotherhood, not just a gang. They helped you and accepted you. They helped fit you into the community. They knew what immigrant kids were experiencing because they had gone through it earlier. The group just absorbed the new kids.

The Family did not have an initiation. You were in by virtue of being with them when there was a fight. This was test enough of loyalty. By reaching out to immigrants and not conducting initiations the group grew to over two hundred members. Sub-groups emerged around the core. Some of these groups developed their own names and identities, but retained their loyalty to The Family. This was demonstrated at a reunion that drew over two hundred guests. The reunion itself was well planned, sophisticated in its detail, and peaceful.

Rolando still has friends from the Family days. These are men who, like him, have gone on to successful mainstream lives.

Q. Was there something in your life that helped direct you away from the gang-banging life?

A. Working with Deb. She was trying her hardest to divert me away from drugs and the gang, but I kept on going back to the same place. But she never gave up on me. When I got busted for selling drugs and carrying a firearm she still never gave up on me. That woke me up and I realized that people cared. At that time I had a vision of where I wanted to be and what I had to do to get there.

Q. How did you get to the point where you were selling drugs and carrying a weapon?

A. Growing up I was exposed to it from my brother and dad. I tried to fit in and be cool. Then it became a habit. Then it went from just being a habit to a lifestyle.

Q. Was it a lifestyle just within your family, or was the gang part of it too?

A. Both, I think. It was all around me.

Within Rolando's community doing drugs was a common behavior. It was considered normal. He said, "Fighting and drugs were part of my daily routine. It was a daily thing to do. You get up, go to school, see your friends, fight, do drugs. It's just part of your life."

Q. How did you feel about that?

A. At first I felt cool, but it was hard. I couldn't go to certain places. I knew where I could and couldn't go. I was constantly watching my back. Going out wasn't comfortable. I had to be with friends.

> I was constantly getting arrested for fighting, vandalizing, and truancy. School was not an important part of my life and it wasn't part of my friends' lives either. I probably missed at least 20 percent of the school days. I would stay after school or go to special classes to make up the work I missed. School wasn't important but graduation was important, and I did graduate.

Rolando said that he was helped by a girl he was going with at the time. "She helped straighten me out," he said. The down side of that experience was that when they broke up his life fell apart again.

Drugs and fighting became the rule. The drugs fed the fighting. "The drugs gave me a false sense of power. They made me feel invincible. I wasn't much of a drinker. I didn't even like drinking, but I did it because it was just what the group did, especially on Friday nights."

Rolando's father was also a drug user, and, when he was using, would become violent toward his wife. He had been a gambler in the Philippines, and while not on drugs back there had, according to Rolando, a tendency toward violent and illegal behaviors.

Rolando remembered that when the family first arrived in Hawaii the family was doing well financially. "My father had a good job as a truck driver," he recalled. The fights between father and mother began to get more terrible. "It was tough," he said, "we could see and hear them." Eventually, Roland's parents separated. Mother moved to Maui with Rolando's youngest sister. To avoid the father's violence they were spirited away by AFY and a counselor from the sister's school. Despite his father's violence toward his mother he wasn't violent toward the children. In fact, said Rolando, he had a minor parenting role. "He was physically present but emotionally detached. If I was around or not didn't really matter to him. He didn't discipline me and my mother didn't discipline me either. Whatever I did was okay with her. When I think about growing up in my family, my dominant feeling was depression. There was no family feeling. You know how families get together and talk at dinner? We never did that. I've been to friends' houses. They went back and forth talking about what they did during the day. I was looking for that in my family. I never had that."

Some of what Rolando believed other kids did in their family had to do with what he observed when he watched TV families. His conclusion that he wasn't getting what he should from his own family came from a mixture of reality and TV.

"In my family we didn't do anything together. Everybody did their own thing. Maybe we would do something with other family members every five years or so. I don't even know my cousins."

With so little to attract him to family life, Rolando was more drawn to his friends and the streets. "My friends made me feel that I belonged somewhere. I felt comfortable with them."

As Rolando was growing up, family life only got worse. From feeling well-provided for financially upon first coming to Hawaii, he said he felt poor as a teenager. Even though both his father and mother worked (she was a packer at a chocolate factory) they couldn't provide what was needed. Even when his father was selling drugs there wasn't enough money because his "ice" habit consumed it.

Rolando was asked if he ever thought that, "This isn't the life I want for myself," or "I don't like this life." He replied, "Not at the time. But looking back, as stupid as it sounds, I'm glad I got busted. If not I don't know where I'd be, probably on the streets or inside. Before I got arrested I thought I'd end up eventually busted, killed, or dead from an overdose. I sure didn't think of living to a ripe old age. Sometimes I thought about suicide, but I knew I didn't have the guts to do it. Even at the darkest times life was still important to me."

When Rolando was asked if he ever thought, when he was in fights, that he could be badly injured or killed, he answered, "Now it scares me but at the time, no. I would just go into the enemy's territory and I didn't think about the consequences, or what could happen to me but now, thinking about it . . . what if they had caught me there and beat me up? Would I still be alive? Now I ask all those questions. It scares me now, but then it never bothered me."

For most people growing up in a middle-class environment, the everyday brawling and violence that Rolando experienced is difficult to comprehend. He believes he was lucky never to be seriously injured. He said, "I knew guys that got badly hurt, guys that were badly beaten, one had his head bashed in with rocks, and another was shot."

Rolando was eighteen when he was arrested. He said, "I was heavy into drugs at the time. It was soon after graduation. I had split up with my girlfriend. I wanted to show her that I could provide. Her family looked down on me because I didn't have a job. They saw me as a freeloader, not doing anything, not having anything to show, so I started selling drugs. I had a habit so I had to support it. I liked having the money and the guns."

A Q-and-A ensued in the interview.

Q. Tell me a little about the guns. How did they come into your possession?

A. People would come by and they didn't have money so they would trade.

Q. How common are guns on the street?

A. Very common. They're all over. They're not hard to find at all.

Q. How about other things besides guns?

A. Everything is easy to find—hand grenades, RPGs, AKs, automatic rifles. I've seen a lot. I'm surprised it doesn't come out. The potential is there. They only need to fall into the hands of the wrong people. The people that have them are not quite there yet. They are not experiencing desperation. They are not at the point that they have to bring it out yet. If people who are in a bad situation have them then it would come out."

Rolando's comments on the weapons that are on the street were chilling to hear, especially coming from him, since he is not one given to hyperbole.

We returned to talk about his arrest when he was eighteen. He said, "The first time I got busted my supplier called me and she told me that they stole her car and the dope was inside the car, so we went to look for it and found the car. We checked the car and found the dope was still there, so we took everything and put it in my car. At that time I was carrying a gun, too. So I took her back to her hotel room. While all of this was going on the housekeeper went in to clean her room and found drugs and money lying on a table, so she called the police. When the woman walked into her room the police were waiting. Stupid me, I was waiting downstairs. I felt something was wrong, but I didn't do anything. The police pulled in behind me and blocked me in. She told them that she was with me. They asked me if they could search the car and I didn't know what to say. That's when they saw all the drugs. They had watched her come in with me so they knew already. They arrested us and took me to OCCC (Oahu Community Correctional Center). That was my first time in jail. It was only one week. I wasn't scared because I knew some people and it made me feel more comfortable.

"My mom and dad bailed me out on borrowed money (I didn't know that at the time), and I didn't know how hard it had been to come up with the money. I took all of that for granted.

"When I got out I went right back into it again with the same woman that got arrested with me. Everything was the same until four months later. I got busted again for the same thing—promotion of drugs and firearms possession.

"Debbie showed up at my first court date and asked the judge to lower the bail. That's why I was able to bail out. She showed up again the second time. My bail this time was something like $125,000. Debbie asked the judge to lower it to $10,000, so after two months in jail I got out again. But, again, I went back into it and my probation officer finally said it isn't working and had me admitted to the Sand Island Residential Treatment Program. I was there for one year, and I did good. But when I came out I went right back into drugs.

"My new probation officer told me, 'You are going to jail or going into another program.' They sent me to Habilitat and I was there for two and a half years.

"I was in a work-training program there, and that's where I think I developed the work habits that I have now. I did good from then on and I kept in touch with Debbie."

When Rolando graduated from Habilitat he had saved only $900 from the work he had done. Getting started again was difficult. He had to put down a deposit of $300, and an additional $300 for one month's rent for one room in a house. This left him with only $300. He struggled with the idea of going back to his old life. However, relationships with people he described as "the positive influences in his life," kept him from slipping back into the drug world.

Rolando found work as a landscaper and mason tender, carrying cement blocks and mixing concrete. The work was hard and he put in long hours but it was rewarding. He bought his first car, a 1986 Honda, and recalled, "I felt proud. It was actually registered in my name."

His life continued to improve. A friend who was a journeyman in the Hawaii Sheet Metal Union offered him a job, and he found that he really liked the work more than anything else that he had ever done. He said, "I was flying to a different island to work. When 9/11 occurred, we couldn't fly because of the restrictions, so I asked the owner of the company to bring me into the union if he couldn't give me work and had to lay me off, so I could collect unemployment and move to Maui where my sister and mother were living. I left with excellent references and when I got to Maui, I found work immediately."

Eventually, Rolando completed a five-year apprenticeship in sheet metal work and became a valued employee of his company. "I was making pretty good money," he said.

His ten-year probation was set to end in 2007, and his life's path should have had all green lights. Not so. A major obstacle was his immigrant status. For his crimes, especially his weapons charge, he was still vulnerable to deportation. In 2003 the Immigration and Naturalization Service (INS) came calling. A nightmare began that would persist for five years.

It was a time during which AFY again became very active in Rolando's life. He had the following to say about this very difficult period and the role that AFY played:

"I didn't expect this. I thought everything was good already because I had changed. If it wasn't for you guys I don't think I would be here today. I would have quit. I told Debbie that I would have given up and accepted deportation. I would have gotten on that plane and gone back to the Philippines. I felt it didn't make any sense to keep on fighting (Rolando was detained in the Honolulu Federal Detention Center for thirteen months, although he had committed no crime, while the effort to prevent his deportation was under way. If he had agreed to removal he would have been free). 'I changed my life and they're doing this to me,' I thought. I didn't want to stay in jail. I already did my time. I had to spend money, money that I didn't have, for a lawyer. But Debbie kept telling me, 'Don't go, don't go, give us a little more time.' She had more faith in me then I had in myself. Debbie kept me strong. Her and my wife. AFY never gave up on me. You did everything you could to keep me here. I thought I had no chance at all. Everyone seemed to feel that way, but because of you guys… " At this point, Rolando's voice trailed off and his eyes filled with tears.

Q. Despite your relationship with Debbie, when you first got locked up in the Federal Detention Center why didn't you get in touch with her?

A. I called her after two months. At first I thought they would let me out. The first time they let me out after three weeks, so I thought the same thing would happen the second time. After they locked me up the second time I started getting letters from my lawyer telling me there was no way I was going to win this case, so, in desperation, I told my wife, 'Could you let Debbie know?' (The lawyer representing Rolando was not a member of the Hawaii Bar, and wasn't required to be since this was a federal issue. AFY subsequently obtained a highly regarded immigration attorney.) Even when I was getting into trouble Debbie always believed in me. She cared about me, and was always there to pick me up when I fell. Her belief in me played a big part in what I was eventually able to accomplish. She was a constant positive force in my life."

Through AFY's efforts and the excellent legal representation we had been able to retain, Rolando was released from federal detention on a $5,000 personal bond, paid by AFY, in June 2004. After three-and- >4-half years of legal wrangling, financed by Rolando and his family, the Department of Homeland Security, U.S. Immigration and Customs Enforcement Division, appearing in U.S. Federal District Court on December 20, 2007, dropped its case for removal against Rolando.

Q. What do you see for your future?

A. I think I have a bright future. I have a good job and my wife has a good job. We have a house, and we own a business providing foster care for older adults. (Rolando is now thirty-four.)

Q. Where do you think you will be ten years from now?

A. I think I'll be working in my field, because I like what I do. Maybe become a supervisor, but not an owner. I like the work side, not the business side, but who knows what will happen in the future?

At the end of the interview, when Rolando was asked if he had anything else to add, he replied, "If I was rich I would contribute to help kids, what Adult Friends is doing." When Sid replied how proud he was of the person that Rolando had become, tears rolled down his cheeks.

Grady

The interview with Grady was conducted one week before he was to turn himself in to begin serving time on a federal drug charge. He expected to serve three-and-a-half years, and was to travel to Oregon and present himself at the facility where he was to do his time. He pled guilty to the charges, and wanted to get started as quickly as possibly so that he could pick up the pieces of his life. He will be located at a low security camp without a fence. His spirits were generally upbeat, and he tried to inject humor into his situation. He said all he needed to do was show up at the facility, knock on the door and say, "Honey, I'm home." Despite trying to make light of his immediate future, sadness kept creeping into his voice.

A year had expired between his conviction and sentencing. He made no effort to run, so, no doubt, he was considered a low security risk. He thought that he may have been assigned to the camp because he has a commercial driver's license and could drive big trucks, which, he believed, were well suited to making deliveries. The thoughts running through his head may have been due more to wishful thinking than about the realities of incarceration. As he was trying to envision his life over the next three-plus years, he was also attempting to see it with as much normalcy as possible.

He said he just wants to do his time and get out. "Hopefully, nobody bothers or provokes me. But you never know if somebody tries to start something." Grady is of medium height and has a stocky build. He is not the kind to back down. Bad behavior would add to his time.

While preparing himself for prison, he sold his lunch wagon business and talked with his two children trying to help them understand what would be happening. He and their mother have been separated for some time, and they live with her. He sold the lunch wagon for less than he paid for it, but had done very well in the business. He also owns a townhouse that he hopes to sell. It is currently rented.

Grady, unlike many of the boys in his gang, who were born in the Philippines, was born in Honolulu. He was thirty-three years old at the time of the interview. He identifies himself as Filipino. While his father is Filipino, his mother is Caucasian. He described his family life growing up as rough. His parents were always working and he had to watch the four younger kids, one brother and three sisters. They range in age from him to the youngest who is twenty-five.

Actually, the man who raised him was his stepfather. His birth father was never married to his mother, and was never part of his life. His mother and stepfather subsequently separated, but not until Grady was an adult. Both of the men were Filipino.

He, Masa, and Rolando were members of the same gang. They lived in the same neighborhood and hung out together. They were friends before he had any sense that the friends he hung with were also a gang. The boys all went to the same middle school and enjoyed playing basketball together. He said that the fights came later. The older boys started The Family about eight months before he got into it.

Grady never went through an initiation. He said, "We never initiated anybody. It was never like that." At first he didn't even know that the group had a name.

"My experience was different than Masa's," he said. "I wasn't being challenged all the time like he was. The fighting went in spurts. Sometimes there would be a lot of fights, and other times we would just cruise, and for long periods of time it would be peaceful. On the other hand, there wasn't a month that would go by that we didn't fight somebody. Our rivals were almost every other gang out there."

In hindsight Grady views the rivalries of the past as, "just plain dumb. It was just so stupid." When the name of a notorious member of a rival gang was mentioned his brow furrowed and he said that at one time they were friends. The boy lived across the street from his cousin and because they were in different gangs they became enemies. (AFY worked with both groups.) In fact the rivalry with that group was quite bitter and feelings ran strong for several years. Even following a period when boys in both groups had grown into young men, dropped their gang-banging and had moved on to "respectable" lives, uncertainty remained among some of the leaders about what would happen if they encountered each other.

An historic get-together of five former antagonists finally occurred at the AFY office and was chronicled by the *Honolulu Star-Bulletin*. Included in the reconciliation were Grady and Masa, and two young people from the rival group, Rey and Jenny, whose stories will be subsequently shared. Excerpts from the newspaper story follow:

"Ten years ago, the small conference room . . . would not have been big enough for the five people sitting and waiting to confront each other, and their violent pasts."

Chaz, Jenny's brother, the fifth person at the meeting, said, "I was so nervous to come here today. I used to be scared to go to school. One of them always used to be waiting for me and wanted to kill me."

He had not seen arch-enemies "Masa," or "Grady," . . . since their fighting days nearly a decade earlier. Yet for "Chaz," the pain and wounds of the past were hauntingly fresh.

"Street fights, drive-by shootings, stealing, gambling, drugs, drinking, gas bombings, racketeering, and harassing others were all part of their daily routine, until Adult Friends for Youth intervened. . . . Where violence and fearing for their safety was once their expectation, goal-setting, education, and peace became their new standards.

"All of them said that in the past they didn't care whether they lived or died because they saw no other options . . . Things changed when they had children of their own."

"We didn't want our own children to be exposed to all the things we had seen," said Grady.

Added Masa, "We know all about the life and—to see our own kids experience it would be the worst thing."

When Chaz was eleven, his mother abandoned the family. "It crushed me. She always said she would come back, and I always hoped she would, but she never did. I met the gang and they were nice to me. That was my family. Doing the crimes seemed like nothing. I had nowhere to go. I was hoping they would put me in jail so

I could stop. We used to drink Mickeys and then fill the glass bottles up with gasoline... gas bomb cars and houses." His sister was never initiated, but her brother's involvement made her an instant target. "People hated me just because I was his sister. Every time I would get off the bus they would be there. They called me horrible names, threw beer bottles at me, and spit at me.'

"Poverty pushed Rey into the gang. 'If people need a pair of new shoes they go buy them. If we wanted a pair of shoes we had to steal them. I feel bad that I took things from people I didn't know, but we didn't have much of a choice. Now, each time I walk in the neighborhood with my daughter, I think about the things I used to do. I am lucky I never saw anyone shot or killed. I do remember ducking as bullets whizzed over our heads in the car.'

"The things these ex-gang members saw seemed unimaginable, except on the big screen."

"Grady admitted gas-bombing six homes in their rival's neighborhood. 'If we could get inside, we would go in the house. Sometimes we would just patrol the hood looking for a fight. (This statement contradicted a statement in the interview that his group didn't go looking for fights. Of course the interview took place seven years later, when reflections may have been based on thinking about the past more as he would have liked it to be rather than the way it actually was.) We would even fight with the school counselors if they got in the way of a rumble. We just whacked them.'

"He said the gang provided acceptance throughout his teen years, a time he was rebelling against the responsibility his single mother expected him to carry. The gang provided the security of numbers. 'Privacy was nonexistent. We couldn't go anywhere alone. If we watched movies, maybe only one guy had a date, but we would all have to go.' Rey added, 'When you stay with plenty people, you're not scared.'

"But the time came to get out. 'When my son was born, I just dropped out and got a job,' Grady said.

At the time the *Star-Bulletin* story ran in 2001, Masa was studying to be a social worker (as we know from his story he became one), Jenny had an administrative position with AFY, Rey was a sous-chef at an upscale restaurant, and was staff trainer for new restaurants that were opened in Hawaii and on the Mainland (he no longer worries about stealing shoes), Chaz was majoring in radiology and raising a family (he subsequently became a skilled sheet metal worker), and Grady was working as the receiving manager for an industrial wholesale company.

When the reunion came to an end, Jenny, according to the article, "Turned to her former enemy, Masa, and said she was sorry for all that had gone before. 'Ten years ago, we would not have been sitting and talking to each other. I used to have a lot of fear and hate. Now I can see him on the street and hug him. It's so different.' Masa replied, 'I love her like a sister now.' Chaz was relieved by the end of the meeting. 'I don't need to wake up scared anymore,' he said. Masa turned to him, 'It's good we closed the final chapter. You can always use another friend.'"

On August 6, 2006, International Forgiveness Day, The Hawaii Forgiveness Project awarded the 2006 Hawaii Hero of Forgiveness Award to Masa and Jenny as "Heroes of Forgiveness, Reconciliation and Peace."

When Grady was asked to describe his adolescence he answered, "It was good, but bad. We had solid friendships, strong bonds, we did things as a group. Having good friends was the best part of being in the group. Bad, because we got into a lot of fights. The violence part I regret, but I don't regret hanging out with this group of guys. Some of us had single moms, or moms that were always working. We hung out with each other to pass the time. A lot of what we did, like playing basketball was normal behavior."

Alcohol and drugs were part of the scene, but, according to Grady, it was different for each person. He said, "I didn't start using until I was older. I was stressing out. I don't know what was wrong with me.

We drank to socialize, not to get ripped. When we drank at the park we went home afterwards. It wasn't like we drank and then went out to start trouble. I can't say that alcohol was a contributing factor to violence. There was a different tolerance level for everybody. For me I think I handled alcohol pretty well. I don't know if some people went out and caused trouble because of it.

"The worst part of the life was when somebody got badly injured. You don't like to see your friend like that. It was a different feeling toward the group we were fighting. When it was happening all you wanted to do was bust somebody up. There was an adrenaline rush. You really don't think about what you are doing. Sometimes I felt bad afterwards, especially if someone ended up in the hospital."

Grady was asked if he ever reached a point in his life when he didn't care whether he lived or died. He replied, "Yeah, when I was on drugs. Everything was like down. The further up I tried to reach the further down I went. This happened to me when I was about twenty years old. I was still friends with the boys, but I no longer considered myself a gang-banger. I really messed up my life. I had a good job. I had a son. I was the supervisor of a warehouse. I had good benefits, including profit sharing. Drugs messed that up."

Q. If things were gong so well, how did you let drugs take over?

A. That's what I think about too, sometimes. How did I let it mess up my life? It came and got me. It started out as a social thing, and then I started doing 'em on my own. That's when it got me. I started spending my money on it, and then the "ice" screwed up my life."

Q. How did you stop?

A. I heard the angels sing. I was into it for about two years. During that time I lost my family, my money, and my mind. I didn't want to die. I stopped cold turkey, out of the blue.

Grady said that he thought about suicide, and even mentioned it as a possibility on a couple of occasions, but that he never really meant it. He posed it as a threat to people close to him just to see if they loved him. "I was never serious, it would have meant automatic hell," he laughed.

From the time Grady was fourteen years old he became relatively independent. He always appeared to want more than just having a job. He acknowledged having an entrepreneurial spirit. "I wanted to own something, and be my own boss. Everyone has their own talents and gifts, maybe this is mine."

After Grady serves his time he knows his biggest struggle will be to avoid the temptation to get back into the big money of drug dealing. He anticipates a lot of pressure to get back into it. He wants to start fresh. It's important for him to preserve his credit, so that when he gets out he will be in a position to borrow money to start a new business. The food industry has always worked out for him. "I always made money selling food." He was a partner in a restaurant at one time and then opened up his own lunch wagon. His first business venture was the restaurant. He said it was like his school. He learned a lot from it. When they lost the lease the business closed. Grady was always a hard worker. He said. "If you want to live comfortably, you've got to work. If you want something you got to go get it. You can't just sit down and expect it to come to you."

Q. When you got into selling drugs how did you look at it? Was it just another business for you?

A. Pretty much, but also to support my habit I began to sell some. When I kicked the habit the addiction to selling was still there. I was addicted to the money. It was a financial boost for me. It was weird. It felt natural to me. Selling comes easy to me. I can't explain it. I guess you could just call me a salesman, but it was illegal. So now I'll just do my time. Then I didn't have much, so I used it to build my capital. Now I can make money by taking out loans. My credit is good. I've learned what I can do as an entrepreneur. I don't need to do illegal things.

Q. You don't think the temptation is going to be there?

A I don't think so. I'm a go-getter. I think I can avoid the temptation. I got a lot of money confiscated from me.

We talked about how involved he was in the gang when a member of his gang shot a member of another gang. He struggled to remember, and then said, "I think the drugs took away some of my memory. People bring up things and I seriously can't remember. There are like blank spots."

When he was selling, it was mostly cocaine. He observed that he hadn't spent most of the drug money. He said, "I always had a job. I also made a lot of money gambling."

Q. The drugs and gambling, is it all part of the lifestyle you were leading?

A. It becomes part of a lifestyle.

Q. Did you ever become part of organized crime?

A. No. It wasn't like the Mafia or anything like that. It was mostly guys who I grew up with who had stuff they could release and asked me if I wanted to sell.

Q. Did you ever carry a weapon?

A. No, but I did get a license to get one, I wanted it for self-defense.

Q. Have you maintained your relationships from 'The Family' days?

A. We talk to each other. As adults we do our own things. We consider ourselves as close, but we don't see each other all the time. But when somebody needs to talk about a problem, like a busted relationship, or needs money to tide them over we help out.

Q. What role did AFY play in your life?

A. They embraced us. They would talk to us as a group and individually. They helped us look at different ways of doing things—better ways. They helped me but I still strayed. They helped others in the group in a good way. AFY changed a lot of people's lives, not only for us but for other groups too. Deb was a big factor in influencing people to not become gangsters. She never gave up. You could always call on her with your problems. Even after high school, we still kept in touch.

Q. Did life change for you and your friends after AFY came into your life?

A There would have been more violence on the street including shoot-outs. Before AFY it was getting out of hand. AFY brought peace to the table. People resolved their differences, and everything kind of faded. That's why for about six or seven years after it was pretty calm.

Q. Do you think it made a difference because we were working with several groups at the same time?

A. I think it did. When we went out with you, other guys started to ask why they couldn't do it too. You took us to do things and provided food. Food was the best part. You also helped me get my first job at the distributorship. That's what turned me around.

Q. What do you regret?

A. The violence. Hurting people. Some people liked that, but I wasn't one of them. Violence and drugs, that's what I regret.

Q. Where do you go from here?

A. [Laughter] From here I go to Oregon for several years to do my time. Come out and start fresh. I still see myself as successful. My goal is to restart my life, legitimately, and go back into business. I was successful with the lunch-wagon business. I got a contract that boosted me up. I was making about two grand a day. It was crazy. When I finish doing my time I plan to come back to Hawaii. My kids are here and I don't want to take them away from their mom. I don't want to leave them. I still want to be part of their lives. It's important to have both a mom and a dad. So far they are both good and haven't gotten into trouble. I told my oldest that I'm going to prison. When he asked me what for I told him that he didn't need to know, but that I did something wrong. I've advised them not to do the wrong things or to hang out with the wrong

> people. I've emphasized the importance of staying in school and studying hard. I plan to stay in touch by phone, but it may be hard because of the time differences.

Grady has had a girlfriend for two years. He said he told her not to wait for him, although she has said that she will. He feels tying her down is not fair, because he was the one who got into trouble and has to pay for it, not her. He said that she shouldn't have to suffer because of him. If she loves him and waits for him that's good for him and he will be happy, but if she can't, he won't blame her. He understands that three years is a long time. "She's sad right now," he said, "but she needs to continue to live her life."

He shared that his goal from the time he was three, was to live a successful middle-class life, to have a house, and to have his children attend good schools.

He dropped out of school at age eighteen to provide for his first child. He received his GED by examination without attending any classes. He feels he is smart in one sense but not in other ways. He has taken responsibility for his bad decisions.

His final words in the interview were, "Life is a struggle, but it's manageable."

Roman

Roman was the flower child of The Family. Perhaps the more antiquated term "Bohemian" fits best. Yet, unquestionably he was a gang leader and a feared fighter. Today he is a balladeer, composing his own music and playing the guitar and singing whenever the opportunity presents itself. When his friend Masa received his master's degree in social work he played at the School of Social Work's graduation exercise.

Now in his middle thirties, he is soft-spoken and spiritual—almost mystic. After living in Nevada and on the West Coast for several years he returned to Hawaii looking more American Indian than Filipino.

In fact, both his mother and father were of Filipino heritage. His mother, who currently lives with one of her four sons on the Mainland, is Ilocano and his father who died in the Philippines in 2001 was Visayan. Roman's parents had a rocky relationship. She moved to Hawaii following a separation from her husband. He eventually followed her, and they even reunited for a short time, but it didn't work out. Roman was in the care of his father after his mother left.

Roman recalled that his father was a businessman in the Philippines who owned several small businesses, and that life was financially comfortable. His father was seldom at home and maids took care of him. They also had a chauffeur.

There were nine children in the family. One brother died in infancy and a second brother died in an Oklahoma prison in 2003 of an alleged heart attack. Roman, who is the youngest of the children, came to Hawaii when he was eight years old. He faced major changes in his life. While he enjoyed a life of some comfort in the Philippines, his mother had modest employment in an Honolulu bakery, a job she would remain in until her retirement at sixty-two.

Roman knew no English when he arrived in Hawaii. He felt poor. In the Philippines he had a driver to take him wherever he needed to go. In Hawaii he had to take the bus. Nevertheless, there were very valuable compensations. He felt surrounded by love. There were always friends and relatives around. He said that the love he experienced made up for not having money.

He recalled that when he misbehaved his mother would smack him, but he never felt abused. On the occasions when he was spanked he felt that he deserved it.

The house often felt too crowded, and too uncomfortable, so the street became his playground. Because his mother left for work early he was on his own and unsupervised most of the time. Whatever he was doing was unknown to his mother and the other adults in his life.

In his family the four boys, but not the three girls, were involved in using and selling drugs. His involvement with The Family began when he was ten. His first experience with drugs began about the same time, because his older brother and his friends were into it. The drug of choice was a most dangerous one; crystal methamphetamine (Ice), which was gaining prominence in the eighties.

The Family was one of four groups that he hung out with at the park. They were just part of the neighborhood, he said. He was never recruited into The Family, they were simply his friends. There were no formal leadership positions. Leaders were those who were looked up to by the other members. Status depended on who was perceived as a tough guy, but, also, on being benevolent. In other words, you were esteemed if you helped out other members when they needed food or shelter. The group helped each other when help was needed. Roman said, "It was a family, even more than the family I was born into. The gang was always there." The gang, he acknowledged, was more important to him and more influential than his birth family.

"From the very beginning the group's intention was to be a gang and to provide protection for its members against the bigger guys, like the Samoans, the troublemakers, and the thieves," he said. "They weren't bothering me," he explained, "but they were bothering my friends. A lot of it started as early as elementary school." When he attended middle school he witnessed Filipinos fighting Filipinos for the first time.

He concluded that gangs, and the conflicts between them, were a neighborhood phenomenon more than an ethnic thing. It appeared to be ethnic because neighborhoods were relatively homogeneous, but if a Filipino lived in a Samoan neighborhood such as the Kuhio Park Terrace public housing project, he would either join the neighborhood gang or suffer the consequences.

It was Roman's belief that gangs are a fact of life in poor minority neighborhoods. "That is the way groups of friends are identified," he said. He felt it was particularly natural for him, because where he grew up in the Philippines there were killings every day. "People were getting shot left and right," he said. "There were plenty gangs in the PI—they were part of the Barcada's tradition."

When asked how he saw a gang as different from a club he responded, "Fighting, crime, killings, drugs, keeping a weapon—all illegal behaviors. Gangs want money and respect. It feels good to have a reputation and a name. Kids in poor neighborhoods are different from more affluent kids, because they don't have the nice homes, the fancy cars, the money. The poor kid may not even have the money to go to a movie. He begins to feel hopeless.

"AFY made a big impact on us," he said. "AFY came into our lives and really showed they cared about us. A big thing to us, that separated AFY from other agencies, was the skin color of staff—Filipinos, Tongans—it taught me that we need more educated people like that. At first we were suspicious of Debbie. We thought she was a cop or from the government. We were also suspicious because she worked with a gang that was one of our biggest enemies. But after awhile we accepted her as a professional. She was there for me when I was in prison. She brought my college work to me.

"The worst part of the gang for me was that one friend was killed, one committed suicide, and one was permanently disabled by a brain injury. It was the fighting, but I don't have flashbacks because of all the things I did in the past. You can't have regrets. It was just the way things were."

When asked if he was ever afraid, Roman answered, "Oh yeah. I was caught walking by myself and got beaten. I was also beaten right inside of a classroom. Four guys from one of our Filipino rivals came right into the classroom and got me."

In response to the question, "Did you ever wait for someone outside of class?" He responded that neither he nor his group had ever done that.

One event that favorably impressed Roman about AFY was, ironically, its effort to reduce the heat between the rival LP/BBI and the police after a member of the LP/BBI group was shot and killed by the police in 1996 when he was found driving a stolen car. AFY requested and received an agreement from the mayor to meet and discuss this issue in an effort to prevent a gang war with the police from erupting. The shooting angered gangs throughout the island, and one gang had already vandalized a police car.

There was little apparent cause for the shooting. Jared Febenito was a frightened sixteen- year-old trying to get away in a car that had been passed from hand to hand. The police claimed that he tried to run down an officer. One radio personality, in a feeble attempt to justify the shooting, chided AFY on air, "Did you know that he had some drugs in his system?" We certainly wondered how a disc jockey had access to this information. Subsequently, the City and County of Honolulu avoided a law suit by arriving at a financial settlement with the family. There were two other boys in the car. One was shot three times and the other escaped unscathed. It was revealed in interviews conducted by AFY that the cop primarily responsible for the shooting had a reputation for harassing suspected gang members, and subsequently left the police force.

Prior to the meeting with the mayor, AFY sat down with the LP/BBI and discussed how an objective and unemotional presentation of the issues could go forward. At AFY's suggestion, a spokesperson for the group would be selected and only he would present the group's grievances. Only five group members would accompany him into the mayor's office. The group subsequently met and agreed on the issues to be presented. The boys sat before the mayor, with the police chief hugging the wall to his left, and the spokesperson proceeded to present, in an orderly and polite manner, the group's concerns regarding the killing of their friend. He did an excellent job. The group was mature and respectful in every way. Unfortunately, their respect was not returned. The mayor made it clear that he was unequivocally uninterested in anything that they had to say, and proceeded to lecture the group on consequences if they engaged in illegal behavior. If it hadn't been for the presence of AFY the meeting would have been an unmitigated disaster, with the group departing in a state of rage that could quickly have inflamed other gangs. The mayor's hard-line position was explained to the group as grandstanding for the media and to calm down the DJ, who had been riding him for a week leading up to the meeting for even agreeing to meet in his "Koa Wood office" with these gang members who were unworthy of any consideration. The meeting itself was accompanied by a media frenzy. Afterwards, we took the boys out for pizza and discussed the political implications of the meeting for the mayor, who was up for election. They learned something about political posturing and calmed down. A crisis was averted.

For some members of the group who were present at the meeting, and those who accompanied them to the city hall (Honolulu Hale), there was an unpleasant aftermath. The authorities did not play fair. Unfortunately, the group did not appear under the niceties of a flag of truce. While the boys may have thought they were invisible amidst the media herd and the mob of people milling about, they were not. Police intelligence was out in force. The boys were right up there on their radar. Several arrests followed. AFY didn't emerge unscathed, either. Following the arrests, some of the boys felt AFY had set them up. It only proved the adage that no good deed goes unpunished.

Not long afterwards, the LP/BBI spokesperson was shot (see account in Masa's story) which sent reverberations throughout the gang community. He and Masa later resolved their differences, which in effect brought the curtain down on the Kalihi gang wars of the era. Relative peace, with some notable aberrations, including a shooting death on the New Year's Eve that began the new millennium, continued for six years.

Roman said that without AFY's presence there would have been a lot of people in prison or killed. "There would have been a lot of bloodshed, that's for sure," he said. He believed that due to AFY's work with the various gangs, trusting relationships had been established that opened doors between the groups and enabled negotiations and mediations to take place.

Fourteen years have passed since the Kalihi peace was established and the friendships that occurred during that gang era have continued. "Relationships are an individual thing," Roman observed. "After a time, when you feel more confident in yourself you don't need the group so much anymore. Most people know who they are. When they were younger they needed the group to feel more powerful. I was always more independent. But, of course when you are in a gang, you always need the group. Even so, I always felt better when I was alone. When I was in the group I felt that people were dependent on me. That's why I felt better when I was by myself and nobody was dependent on me and I could go my own way."

He saw the lyrics to his song, "The Lighted Ones," as a message of hope. He said, "People always saw the worst part of them, the negative side. They didn't see the positive. They saw us as druggies, gangsters, or troublemakers."

Q. When people saw you like that what do you think they wanted to do about you?

A They wanted to get rid of us. "The Lighted Ones" was a way to communicate that there is humanity here, that we are people who are struggling with our identity and who we want to be. That we can only survive through a collective brotherhood where we can help and support each other."

Of all Roman's experiences he was most remorseful about Michael's beating and subsequent paralysis. He reflected, "Debbie would bring him to group sessions. He liked to play music and I played music. What happened to Michael was tragic. It changed his whole future."

When asked about his own future he replied, "I think I am where I'm supposed to be. I have a music recording and a music video. It's all my own music. I don't know whether I will ever be able to support myself through music but I like to think that there is that potential. My life is simple and I don't need much." He was asked what he believed would happen if AFY closed its doors and went out of business. He looked shocked at the question. He then went on to answer it. "I think there would be a lot of troubled and confused kids out there. You are opening a lot of doors for kids that would otherwise remain closed. AFY provides understanding and brings hope and opportunity. It's different from other programs because it reaches out to kids. You become one of them instead of expecting them to go to you." Even as he was speaking he became a little agitated at the question and asked, "Why would you do that? It doesn't make any sense. You guys do so many good things, why would you want to shut down? I can't find the right words to say how much you guys are doing for the community."

Roman's strong words of support prompted a follow-up question. "What do you believe would have happened to you if we never came into your life?" He responded, "I think I would have been in prison or maybe dead, and maybe the same would have happened to my friends, or maybe we would have lost our minds. There are a lot of crazy people out there."

Unlike some of his friends, Roman never considered suicide. His life was always precious to him. He felt he always had good support, including support from AFY. Given that he considered life as meaningful he was asked, "So when you got into fights, did it ever worry you?" He answered, "Yes, it worried me. I worried about the consequences. I fought to survive—to defend myself. I know I was different from many of my friends. Some of them didn't care whether they lived or died. We talked about how we felt and about family, sometimes late into the night. I felt pain for them. It hurt to know how they were feeling, but at the same time I felt closer to them because they respected me enough to share their emotions with me."

The Lighted Ones

The sun has finally risen
It's time to meet the lighted ones
That guides me through the day, through the night
So I shook, I shook my brothers' hands
'Cause it's the meaning for us lighted ones

Oh! Lord will you bless us
Oh! Lord will you bless us
If we may break the law
I guess this is the only way for us to survive
To share what we've got deep in our hearts

People say we ain't got nothing' in life
'Cause my brothers and I always fight
They don't understand
Where my brothers and I are comin' from
They treat us as if we ain't human
But deep inside our hearts
There's a heart hard as diamond

The sun slowly falling down
As for us we stood our ground
I guess we can't stay forever
But our name is always remembered
And so I shook and I shook my brother's hand
That's the meaning for us lighted ones
Respect, respect everyone

The sun has finally risen
It's time to meet the lighted ones
Put on the cross close to my heart
That guides me through the day, through the night
So I shook, I shook my brother's hands
'Cause it's the meaning for us lighted ones

Sarah

Sarah was born in Long Beach, California. Her mother was of mixed ancestry, Hawaiian, Chinese, and German. Her father was full Samoan. The family moved to Hawaii, and straight into the Kuhio Park Terrace Public Housing Project, when she was ten years old. She grew up at KPT and didn't leave until she was nineteen. She remembered very little about life in Long Beach except that she knew the boys in her family were gang-bangers, and remembered a lot of yelling between her mother and father. Her mother had family in Hawaii and wanted to get away from her husband, and, according to Sarah, wanted to start a new life for herself. When they came to Hawaii her mother fell in love with the weather so they just ended up staying.

Sarah has an older sister and two brothers. She also has a half-sister and a half-brother from her father's other family, who live in Missouri.

At the time the family lived in Long Beach, despite her knowledge of family violence and involvement in gangs, she remained aloof from the problems. That all changed when she moved to Hawaii and got swept up into alcohol, drugs, and gang life that were endemic to the housing project.

Adult Friends for Youth became acquainted with Sarah when she was thirteen. The agency, at the time, was working with three gangs of a generational gang known as the Sons of Samoa at KPT; The Juniors, Peewees, and Baby Gangsters. As part of an effort to help the boys become reacquainted with their cultural roots and establish pride in their heritage, Mac Schwenke introduced them to Samoan music and dance. One summer evening, a variety show featuring acts of young people who had completed KPT's summer recreation program highlighted their talents before family and neighbors. The boys, who were trained by Mac, were the stars of the program. The audience leaned forward in great anticipation as the beat of Samoan drums and timpani filled the room. Parents and neighbors who knew the boys only as troublemakers were amazed at their brilliant performance. Tears and smiles filled the room. Parents were for the first time proud of something that their sons had accomplished.

At the reception, following the performances, little Sarah pulled on Sid's shirt and pleaded that since we were helping the boys why couldn't we help her group of girls as well, and so we did.

During the interview, she recalled that the girls were jealous that Mac was meeting with the boys and that they were getting all the attention, but she couldn't recall approaching Sid and insisting that the girls needed help. She explained, "My brains at that time were lost, because I was smoking so much weed." She began smoking cigarettes when she was eleven, and got heavily into alcohol when she was about fourteen. She became pregnant that same year by the boy who eventually became her husband. She was talked into an abortion by her mother and a staff member of another agency.

Sarah described herself at the time as being so out of it that she didn't care about anything. "I didn't know what to do with myself. I drank all the time. I would just drink, drink, drink, every day. I drank because I just didn't want to feel the pain. Drinking made me have happy thoughts, and that's all that I wanted. I just wanted to have happy thoughts." She felt conflicted about the abortion. On the one hand she wanted to have the baby. On the other hand she knew that she couldn't afford the baby, financially, and that she was still a baby herself. "I know at that time that I was in no position to care for a baby, but I still rebelled against my mom. By blaming her I didn't have to take responsibility. My boyfriend certainly didn't want to be a daddy. He was only four months older than me. I didn't want to go home and after that I stayed out three or four nights a week."

Sarah spent time with three different gangs from time to time. One group of older girls came together because they had a common interest in singing. Her sister, a year older, was a member. Sarah was the baby of the group. The girls took on the mantle of being the toughest girl gang in the community. On one occasion AFY attempted to pull two girl gangs together for a television interview. The other group said that they wouldn't come to the office if the KPT group was present. The KPT girls did the interview, which revealed much about their perspective on life. Many of its members had already dropped out of school and they said so to the interviewer. When the interviewer asked why they had left school the girls responded, "What's the point of going to school if you don't think you will be alive to graduate?"

In addition to the gang of older girls, Sarah said, "We had our little girls' group that started out in school. We knew each other but didn't get close until we were in high school. Originally there were only four members and we named ourselves by the initials of our first names."

Sarah's third gang was the all-male, except for her, Baby Gangsters. She explained, "Each group had a tomboy and I was kicking around with the BGs. One day I was playing around with them and they said that I might as well be one of them, but that I would have to be jumped in. There were four of them. They beat me up for about a minute. I remember that day vividly. I wouldn't want to go through that again. They beat me up like I was a guy. They never had any remorse. One of the boys finally stepped in and said that was enough. He reminded them that I was a girl. They treated me like one of the guys. There was no sexual involvement."

When she reflected back on what she called the "little girls' group," she said, "At the beginning it was all fun. The bad times were when you had nothing. There are times when you need help and you reach out to someone in your family and there's no one there. You feel like your world is ending. I felt like that a couple of times. I hold things in and sometimes feel like I'm going to burst, and then I explode. I try not to but I can't help it. The group was my outlet. We would go to other places and cause trouble just to make our name known, because now there were nineteen of us. We called ourselves a gang. We saw ourselves that way and wanted others to see us that way." To confirm that they were a gang they even wore a colored rag, just like the boys.

"We would go by a rival housing project and call the girls out. We would taunt them to meet at a certain place to fight. We did all kinds of dangerous stuff and didn't even think about the consequences. No one cared because our lives were already so awful. Drugs and alcohol just added to the 'I don't care' attitude. We would go on beer runs where we would grab beer and just run.

"I feel that I've been around drugs my whole life. I've never sold them but my brothers did. While drugs give you that 'I don't care feeling,' some also make you paranoid, like you feel that someone is after you. To be honest, I loved the highs, but feeling paranoid wasn't nice. There were two separate highs. The first relaxes you and the second numbs you. It felt good, you don't have any worries. Your mind is so blank. You're in la-la land."

Seven years after Sarah's father abandoned the family, he showed up on their doorstep. She was seventeen. He moved in and stayed. At first she was shocked and happy that he returned. When he first left she felt the family was better off without him. She didn't feel hurt or abandoned, because he wasn't around that much anyway, and when he was present there was so much turmoil that she avoided him. Due to his frequent absences her mother had assumed the roles of both mother and father, so his departure left no hole in her life. The only feeling she could recall having at the time was that she felt free.

When he came back into her life, she attempted to establish a relationship with him, but after awhile gave up. "I just didn't bother," she said.

Her mom was so happy to have him back that she let him take over, and he had no problem attempting to assert his authority over the family. Sarah said, "He beat us. We were all very scared of him. I do have a soft spot for him, but at the same time I hate him. He was a drunk. He held a job for a little while, maybe three years or so, but it didn't last. Back then he was also doing drugs." He still lives with Sarah's mother, "But," Sarah said, "No one has anything to do with him."

Sarah described her mother as, "A boring lady. She doesn't like to make friends. She's a loner. She lectures kids on doing the right thing, but couldn't even influence her own kids. She tried to discipline us but she was weak. We took over. Besides, she worked, so she was hardly ever home. When my father came back he tried to change things. If we weren't home he came looking for us with his belt."

Her mother worked as a security guard at the housing project on the graveyard shift when the children were young. Ironically, she subsequently obtained a certificate as a drug counselor and was employed for well over a decade as a drug counselor for a prominent international organization. Sarah smiled at the irony of it all. "She is in denial about all the drugs in her own family," Sarah said. Sarah's brothers sell drugs to support their own habits, and her sister did prison time for drugs and probation violations. Sarah described her family as, "very dysfunctional. It isn't nice."

For the most part her friends have survived, and are doing well. Sarah has been steadily employed for a number of years in a responsible position with a car rental agency.

Much of the credit for breaking away from the gang lifestyle for her and her friends goes to AFY she said. "AFY definitely influenced me. I didn't know you could do good in the world until McKay came into our life. He did all the right things, even knowing that we were such irritating little kids. We felt that he loved us. He was different from the other adults in our lives. He really cared about us. His expressions of support and love were something we never felt from our parents. McKay was like a second family to us. He took us places and talked to us. He was like a father figure. Debbie and Simi also influenced us. Debbie was like a role model. Because of her, at one time, I thought about being a social worker. I felt so much love coming from AFY. Being accepted for who I was and not being judged was a new experience for me."

Sarah saw the work that Mac and Simi were doing with their gangs. She said they communicated to the boys that life could be better, that they had choices. "They gave the boys hope and made them feel that they were capable of achieving a better life. They made them feel that they were worth something. Growing up in a project made us feel like we were nothing." She sees gangs as environmental.

"If you don't have anything you turn to the streets. If you don't have positive role models you turn to what you know."

Sarah received her high school diploma through the competency-based adult education (C-Base) program of the Hawaii Department of Education that Mac helped her enroll in. She still has hopes of continuing with her education at some point.

At this time, however, she feels that her life is on hold. Her husband is currently incarcerated in Oklahoma for a drug-related probation violation. When they got married in 2004 he had only been out of prison for a week. "For the next two years," she said, "he was doing good, and then he wanted fast money." They lived together for three years. He went back into prison in 2007.

Sarah said, "He's been in the system since he was sixteen. He's now thirty. He also grew up in KPT, and was a member of the Baby Gangsters. It has been very difficult for me. I live day by day. I have faith. My work keeps me going. Life is stressful. I still live with my parents. My sister moved in with us when she got out of prison. We all moved out of the projects when I was nineteen, and I don't associate with anyone from my past. I always wanted to go back to school, but right now I can't do that. I have to support my mom, so I need the income. With my husband in prison and having to take care of my mom it really stresses me. I can't do everything at one time, so I just do my best. Sometimes I think I just want to be a bad girl again. There is a constant struggle going on inside of me. Sixty percent of me wants to stay on the right path and do good, and then there is the other forty percent that wants to let loose, drink, and not care about anything. Just go buck wild. What keeps me strong is waiting for my husband for us to build our own future. I don't want to live with my parents anymore. I want to get my own place, my own car. I've got to believe that when he gets out things will be better. We communicate every day. He tells me I don't have to worry or cry anymore. When he gets out he will go into a federal halfway house. I still have a long wait."

Malefati

At the time of this interview Malefati was thirty-one years old, married and the father of three girls. The oldest, sixteen years of age, was his wife's daughter from a previous relationship. The other girls are six and three. He hasn't lived in the hood for several years. The interview was a step back in time for him.

He had been a member of two groups within the Kuhio Park Terrace SOS intergenerational gang. He was first a member of the BGs, and at thirteen was jumped into the Peewees. When asked when his relationship with the Peewees came to an end, he replied, "I don't remember it ever coming to an end. It's still 'we're the boys,' but now I've got other obligations. The gang identity is still there, but in a positive way. It is more like that old gang of mine. A group of friends hanging out together. The last time we got together was about a month ago when our friend died. He died from obesity and related health problems."

While Malefati was born in Hawaii, both parents were born in Samoa. They met in Hawaii. He described their marriage as being a "rocky road." "They are very different people," he said. "She is a college graduate and he was a warehouse worker. She was employed by the state in a very responsible job that sometimes took her to Washington, D.C." His father was very jealous of her and didn't like her traveling. By the time Malefati was two years old he had forced her to quit. The family's financial situation turned downward from there and never recovered.

Malefati was very bitter about the family's poverty and the difficulties he endured because of it. Much of his anger is directed at his father who he referred to as, "an abusive alcoholic." His mother suffered "a lot" of physical abuse that Malefati, his three sisters, and two brothers were witness to. They were also victimized, but Malefati's most painful memories were of the beatings his mother suffered. He said, "Sometimes he threatened the kids to make her more compliant. He was a compulsive bully who demanded that everything be done his way. He was like a drill sergeant."

Malefati has great love and admiration for his mother, because, "with all the crap she had to put up with she still had the strength to keep the family together." Malefati's family is now scattered. Three children live in California, two are in Hawaii and one is in Samoa. They ranged in age from twenty-eight to forty at the time of the interview. He is second-youngest. He appears to be closest to the women in his family. Not only does he love and feel protective of his mother, he is closer to his sister who lives in Samoa than to his other siblings. He also felt very close to his grandmother in Samoa before she died. His grandmother, in the Samoan tradition of raising a grandchild after her own children have left the nest, raised his sister, almost from the time of her birth. "From the time we met we had a special bond. We just clicked from the very beginning," he said. His sister is married and has four children.

While most of the youth who were born and grew up in KPT have a distinct local pidgin style of speaking, Malefati's speech is indistinguishable from that of well-born youth. He attributes it to his efforts to cover up how much he hated his life. In addition to speech he also uses comedy as a shield. His intelligence jumps out in any interaction and belies the fact that he has only a high school education.

He was very conscious of his poverty. He knew that other people had much better lives and he aspired to cross over and be like them. His window to that other world came through television. He said he watched TV shows like "Silver Spoons" and "Family Ties" and other family-oriented shows and thought, "Why do they have everything and we have nothing." There were a number of "whys" that came to mind. "Why do I have to steal to eat and live, and they don't? Why do they have money and I don't?" He began to analyze his life and the lives he experienced through TV. One of his conclusions was that there is a difference between the way he and his friends sounded and the way the TV characters sounded. So, he concluded, if I talk the way they talk then I could have what they have.

"As a kid I really wanted more," he said. "When I watched those shows it really hurt. I felt they lived an awesome life, and I deeply resented them. When I went to school and sang about the land of the free and home of the brave, I asked myself where was the free. I thought you gotta be brave to live here because there ain't nothing free." Malefati said it was probably about fifth grade when he realized that there was a privileged world and he wasn't part of it.

He honed in on other differences between his family and the TV families. He became aware that his family did not eat together. He commented, "As far as sitting down as a family and having a conversation about how everybody's day went it never happened." His mother and father came and went. "The kids just ate what was available," he said. "If there was no food we didn't eat. We would wait until we went to school next day to get free school lunch. There were times I went through the trash bins because I was so damn hungry. Once, I literally looked into the trash bin, saw some bread in there, picked it up, dusted it off and ate it."

He didn't see much difference between his poverty and the poverty of his friends. If they had food they would share with him and he would share with them. He felt that they were all in the same boat.

Although his parents both worked, money was always short. There were a total of seven mouths to feed, and on top of that relatives frequently visited and lived with them, which only added to the family's financial woes. Malefati's father worked at menial jobs as a warehouseman, and in the hotel industry, while his mother, despite her education and experience, worked, at different times, as a janitoress and at fast-food restaurants.

Income went mostly to rent and utilities. "There were times when my parents argued about what bills to pay," he said. "There was a lot of physical and emotional abuse. My father wanted my mother to wait on him hand and foot. He didn't like the idea of my mother going to work. It seemed like he didn't want to face the reality that there wasn't enough money coming into the household. Because of his insecurity he couldn't accept the idea that she made more money than he did, and could have made even more if he hadn't forced her to give up her state job, or that when he wasn't working that she was the sole bread winner in the family. When she worked for the state she was 'hot.' When he met her and they started to go out it was like he hit the jackpot. He completely dominated her, but divorce was never an option. I asked her about it once, and she said it wasn't anything that she would have seriously considered because in the Samoan culture divorce was a disgrace and would have brought shame on her family name. As for me, I am proud to be Samoan. I love my culture. It is always God first and respect. The biggest weakness is not being able to adapt. Not being able to look outside of the Samoan culture, and not finding a way to make the culture work in the outside world. That frustrates me.

"The black middle class mimicked white society in many ways. It had its own social institutions that were mirror images of white fraternal organizations. They had a professional class and black colleges. They aspired for the most part to be fully integrated into American society. The black-power movement was an angry response to being blocked from achieving that goal. It's sad to say, but too many Samoans want handouts. It isn't that Samoans don't dream about something better. It's just that there are too few who will fight to achieve their dreams. Too many get up hoping that God will bless them and their problems will be solved."

The gang was Malefati's way of getting out of the house. In the early years mainland families brought the gangs to the projects. It was either the Crips or the Bloods. If you lived at KPT it was the Crips. At Kam IV housing it was the Bloods. The Halawa H-Mobs were Crips. Malefati said, "The Mayor Wright boys jumped in with Kam IV so they became Bloods. Kam IV were our biggest rivals."

Malefati recalled that when he was ten years old he was arrested for the first time for shoplifting a Halloween costume. He reasoned that if he couldn't afford to buy it, it was okay just to go and steal one. He was placed in a cell in the "old Kalihi Police station" and recognized names of the older boys on the benches and the walls. When he put his own name down he believed that jail was his future. Later when he got into his first gang fight he predicted, "Fight, jail, and pretty soon dead."

When he was first introduced to AFY's McKay Schwenke by some of the older boys, he thought that Mac "was some kind of con artist." He obviously must have something up his sleeve, Malefati thought, why else would he take the boys to the beach, and do other "fun stuff," if he wasn't out to use them in some way. Malefati reasoned, "Okay, I'll use you too. I'll play your game as long as I get what I want out of it, and then it's so long, sucker. But then I found he talked to us about things that we were interested in. Our conversations became important to me. He helped me believe that doors I felt were closed to me, because of who I was, were really open, if I wanted them to be. I remember talking to him while we were sitting on the sand, and I began to think that even if the door was closed it wasn't locked. He said that it was up to me if I wanted to turn the handle and open the door. I heard stuff like that all the time on TV, but this time it was different. This time it was a person who I knew and trusted telling me this. It made a real difference, besides it helped that he was Samoan. This was a guy who I felt really cared about me and my friends. He was someone who really wanted us to be safe. I thought here is this guy who is Polynesian, and I admired the way he presented himself, and the way he looked and where he lived that he must be doing good. The fact that he actually went to college and got a degree was something. Even though helping us was his job it was clear to us that he really enjoyed doing it. He was working with children, but instead of working in some nice comfortable place he came to work in the hood. I thought when you got a college degree you were offered a silver platter, but when you turned it in for a paper plate you were my kind of guy. With Mac and Simi it was like two Polynesian adults looking out for Polynesian kids. When kids start breaking rules when they're young they get in the habit of breaking rules, and as they grow up they break even more and bigger rules. Mac and Simi helped prevent the inevitable from happening.

"AFY was successful with me because I had the want and drive to have a better life. AFY smoothed the road out for me. It didn't work for everyone. Some of my friends had a different mentality.

They believed that they were always going to be in the hood and the system. When Mac helped me see that the doors weren't locked I believed him. Others see the doors are forever locked. They develop a victim mentality. Before someone can walk through the door they have to believe they are capable of walking through it.

"Being in the gang is all about violence, power, and control. The stories about these mean bullies taking kids' lunch money are all true. It was that kind of life. By the time I was thirteen, I had already been arrested three times. The gang would hijack people, not only at school, but at bus stops and on the street. If you looked like you had money we were going to take it from you. My arrest record kept on growing until we met Mac and Simi. I looked forward to the one to two times a week we met with them. I tried to keep my nose clean. I wanted to make sure that nothing interfered with my going out on our outings."

When asked if his parents knew he was in a gang, Malefati responded, "My mother knew something was going on but avoided pushing the issue with me. My father was hardly around, and I had the sense that he didn't care one way or the other. On the other hand he did care when I was in a fight. He participated in the Golden Gloves, so fighting was a big thing with him, and being the bully that he was when I got into fights he would make me go back and finish them off. Finish it meant winning. I had to go back, and he would go to witness it personally.

"I used drugs, mostly weed, from time to time," Malefati noted, "but it was a social thing, I never got hooked. I also sold a little for pocket money. The worst thing about being in the gang was the fighting. The best was the friendships, and the feeling of family. I enjoyed the good feeling of hanging out with my brothers just joking and drinking. I miss that part of it."

Malefati has moved on with his life and is strict with his girls. He expects all of them to go to college and get good jobs. He has the same expectation of his four nieces.

He received his big-rig trucking license through Leeward Community College and subsequently became an instructor. Driving large trucks has been his career for several years. He currently is a big-rig truck driver for the State of Hawaii and has started to dabble in politics. He worked part-time as a legislative aide during a recent legislative session after his normal work day was over. His legislative experience has generated cynicism. He feels that too many legislators are in it just for themselves, and that there is very little sense of the public good. He believes he can do better and is considering running for office himself. When that may occur he isn't sure, but he said he is discouraged when he drives through the old neighborhood of Kalihi and "sees the same old crap."

Rey

Rey is thirty-five years old. He has an eighteen-year-old daughter who recently graduated from high school. He was a young father in love with a beautiful girl when their baby was born. They never married. Eventually, they drifted into their careers and moved apart. She, subsequently, married but Rey never has.

He developed an interest in cooking through his father, and became increasingly skillful as he grew older. He became a self-taught chef of some renown. While in his twenties he achieved the position of sous-chef of a Honolulu fine dining restaurant that branched out to Maui, Hawaii Island and the U.S. Mainland. He went from place to place, helping to set up the new restaurants as they emerged. Unfortunately his compensation fell short of the work demanded of him and the responsibilities he shouldered for the company. He became discouraged and reluctantly relinquished his prestigious position for a job with a four-star restaurant that paid more but reduced him to becoming a line cook. He is very frustrated because there is no room for creativity and feels his talents are underutilized. He continues to work at the job while dreaming the dream of many chefs, having his own restaurant. He decided on the name long ago—Rey's Place. Even so, if someone offered him the opportunity to manage a fine dining restaurant as the executive chef, he said he would grab it.

During our discussion, he confessed that he felt depressed on his birthday because he was alone. His daughter "was doing her own thing," and there was no one with whom to celebrate. Rey, despite his talent and the respect that he has earned, exudes an aura of melancholy.

Rey's father recently retired from a janitorial job and returned to the Philippines to live, which, Rey said, was always his plan. His mother is a housekeeper at a hospital and remains in Hawaii. Rey has three older sisters. His parents came from South Luzon, about six hours south of Manila. Rey visited the Philippines twelve years ago. His family moved to the United States when he was nine years old, and he became naturalized as a citizen with his mother when he was thirteen years old. His father never became a citizen.

Rey said he was excited to come to Hawaii, but he didn't know any English. Learning a new language was very difficult for him. He still speaks with a distinguishable accent.

When the family first arrived, life was very difficult. They lived with another family in a very crowded two-bedroom apartment in the big city, which was in sharp contrast to living on a farm in the Philippines.

Rey said that his family was not very close. There was very little communication and the family did not eat meals together. (It appears that failure of families to eat together is a common denominator among youths interviewed for this book. The lack of family cohesiveness seems to be a strong influence for youths to turn to relationships and friends outside of the family.) Rey attributes family indifference as an important factor that drew him into a relationship with his gang. When he was in the eighth grade, a prominent member of the group invited him to hang out with them. Rey said, "I didn't know they had a name, they were just the boys in the neighborhood. All of us just grew up together. We all went to the same school and hung out in the same park. We got into fights with a lot of different gangs including other Filipino gangs and Samoan gangs. One gang wasn't even in Kalihi. They were another Filipino gang in Waipahu, another predominantly Filipino community about eight miles away.

"Mostly, the fights were territorial. For the street gangs it was about protecting territory and the name. Fighting was nothing new for me. Even before I became part of the gang I had been in plenty of fights."

Q. If you were asked to join the gang and you were already hanging out with the boys what was the point of going through an initiation?

A. It was just part of the ritual of being in a gang—to show loyalty and respect. It was to show you could take beatings and being mobbed by other gangs.

Q. Did you know when you were going to be initiated?

A. No. It was a surprise. They told me if I wanted to be in the group I had to do it. In my case it wasn't that big of a deal compared to what I saw other guys go through. I saw worse. Mine was short. I only had a few bruises. That was about it. I got kicked and punched.

"After I became one of them," Rey said, "I started to smoke and drink and stay up late and get in trouble in school. I got into more fights and got arrested. My first arrest was for joyriding. One of the boys had stolen a car and six of us were in the car when we got pulled over in a shopping center. The officer had a flashlight on us and had his gun out. He asked us to step out of the car. For some reason he thought I was the leader and he threw me to the ground, and stepped on me and handcuffed me. I didn't resist except I didn't want to go on the ground. I didn't even know the car was stolen. Maybe I didn't want to know. They made me stay on the ground face down for at least fifteen minutes. They told me not to move, and the whole time the police officer had his foot on my back. I was the last one they put in the blue and white. I was fourteen at the time and was really scared. They took us to the Pearl City police station. It was about eight or nine o'clock that night when we got arrested and it took another two hours for them to process us. Then they called our parents. My mom and dad, and my older sister showed up. They were outraged and hysterical. 'What the hell were you guys doing stealing a car?' That about sums up their reaction. That was the only time I was arrested for auto theft, but I was arrested for a lot of other things such as burglary and theft. I did steal other cars but never got arrested for it."

Rey acknowledged that his parents had no control over him. "They just kept telling me, 'Don't do that again.' There was no physical punishment."

"Things sometimes got really scary," said Rey. "The scariest times were when the whole group was drinking and doing drugs, because anything could happen then. We would push each other into mischief. Other times, when someone called the group together, you already knew something was going to happen. Fighting was always scary because you never knew what to expect, whether you were going to get beaten, stabbed, or shot. Sometimes you didn't want to go to school by yourself, or go out of your house, or walk down the block without someone with you. You didn't know if there was another gang around the corner or cruising. It was always scary. I was always afraid to go places by myself. You never knew if someone would recognize you.

"Each gang had its own territory at school. I carried either a switchblade or butterfly knife. I usually didn't carry a gun, but at one point I carried a .38 special to school after my friend died. People kept bats and various sharp objects in their cars.

"School was a scary place, because you never knew if someone was waiting for you outside of class. One time I was in my English class and four guys from one of our rivals were waiting outside for me. They hung out by the class and had seen me when we went out for recess. After class they charged me. A girl had warned me, but what was I supposed to do? My first thought was just to stay in the classroom, but then I decided to step out. I couldn't show fear. If I did they would keep picking on me. They left me with a black eye, and we retaliated after that."

Upon hearing Rey's tale it was possible to imagine similar scenarios playing themselves out in schools and neighborhoods across the country, where schools are battlegrounds and students are fighting for survival. News stories confirm that sometimes the outcomes are deadly.

Adult Friends for Youth doesn't need to be reminded by the media. It has experienced the deadly impact of gang warfare and the too-easy access to weapons up close. On the New Year's Eve ushering in the new millennium a young man from one of our groups, high on drugs, shot and killed another boy with whom we were also working. The victim was well on his way to making healthy changes in his life. It was a personal tragedy for AFY as well. Debbie was working with both of the young men. The boy who did the shooting was convicted of manslaughter and sentenced to ten to twenty years. He was eighteen years old at the time and hardly knew what he was doing. The gun was being shot off almost as if it was part of a fireworks display.

On a Mainland speaking trip in 2009, four AFY staff (including Deb) visited this young man at the Saguaro Correctional Center in Arizona (Hawaii warehouses its prisoners at this private Corrections Corporation of America facility halfway between Phoenix and Tucson in what can best be described as an air-conditioned hell in the desert). We were his first visitors in nine years. He was stunned and in tears when we showed up. Deb has stayed in touch, through letters, all of these years, and will continue communication until his expected release in 2013. She hopes to help him ease back into the community at that time, although since he isn't a citizen, it is likely that he will be deported to the Philippines.

Rey recalled that his gang had about twenty members. He said, "The leaders didn't have titles but became leaders through respect gained by their seniority and ability to scrap. Meetings were called by the leaders and passed by word of mouth from group member to group member. You have to remember that this was before cell phones and the Internet were in common use."

While we were talking, Masa, a former bitter rival, walked in. The two men embraced each other as comrades who had suffered on the same battlefield and had survived. They shared bits of information about their families and reminisced a little about the past.

Rey acknowledged that sometimes members argued among themselves about whether they should be fighting certain groups, especially when members had friends in those groups from going to school together or living in the same neighborhoods. "I sometimes questioned why I was doing this thing. It was like, you know me, I know you, so what's the point. When you get right down to it the point often had nothing to do with right or wrong, it was all about being loyal to your group."

In the course of our conversation Rey struggled hard to come up with what the good parts of being in the gang were beyond the friendships. He said he wanted to get out and thought about why he got into it in the first place. He has regrets about ever having been in the gang, but those regrets seem to be afterthoughts. At the time he was heavily involved in the lifestyle. As he matured, and as his ambitions for a better life began to form, he began to think about getting out, but by that time he felt that there was no way out. He had never jumped anyone out, because no one had ever tried to get out. He said he eventually got out by spending less time with the group after his daughter was born and he had the responsibility of taking care of his family. What Rey didn't realize, but what AFY understood, was that other members of the group had also started to drift away to pursue their own individual lives separate from the gang. In fact by the time he drifted away only two members of the group still maintained a gang-banging mentality. While friendships were still loosely maintained, group cohesion had significantly declined, and for the most part the gang identity ended, except for the two who were being left behind.

Subsequently, a clash emerged between the two factions. Several members of the group asked to meet with AFY. The problem they faced was the attempt by the two to bring them into a fight, which they had instigated. The boys expressed guilt at abandoning their friends, when they had always been there for them. They talked about the love they had always had for each other and the difficulty they were having in resisting the pressure that was being brought to bear on them. We talked about love being a two-way street, and asked, if the two really did have their best interests at heart would they be asking them to do something that would put them in harm's way? Further, we wondered if it wouldn't be helpful to the two if they joined the boys who had moved on, instead of the other way around.

The story has a happy ending. The boys met together and shared that the past was the past for them and that they were not going back to a lifestyle that had already ended. Their two friends resisted change for awhile, distanced themselves from their old friends, and attempted to recruit younger boys into a new gang. It wasn't long, however, before they also gave it up. These two former comrades no longer see each other. One went on to a successful career as a skilled union craftsman in the construction trades, married, and has two children. The second, as far as we know, seems still to be struggling to obtain a stable life.

Rey said that Debbie and AFY were very influential in the changes that the gang made. He said that she gave them the opportunity to have fun outside of the "gang stuff." He said, "She challenged us to think. She asked questions about what we were going to do beyond the gang-banging, what we wanted to do with the rest of our lives, if we were planning to graduate from high school, what would happen if we got shot or hurt. She made us think about options outside of the gang. She made us think about the future. Before she discussed these issues with us, I didn't ever think about graduating from high school. The gang was the thing, and the boys just dropped out. Not only for our gang but all the gangs. When I was in the gang I didn't think about how my life was going to end up. I only thought about the moment. I just lived in the here and now. I did things recklessly. I just didn't care. I thought I would get shot or killed or end up in prison. Nobody in my family talked to me about what I was going to do in the future. Debbie made me believe that I had potential for a different kind of life—a better life. My first goal became graduation from high school."

Debbie took the group to interview for jobs at a drugstore chain. The goal was to get into warehouse work where they could employ their brawn. Each was given an aptitude test. Rey scored in the top percentile in math and was offered a position as a cashier. He was proud of his achievement, and for the first time really began to understand his capabilities. His math skills were put to good use as planner and buyer for the restaurant when he was sous chef.

"Debbie made it easier for the boys to get out of the gang. If you guys hadn't come along we probably would have been gone." When asked what he meant by "gone," Rey replied, "I would have been in jail or dead. You guys became our second parents." Indeed we were. After Rey's girlfriend gave birth, Sid and staff member Terry Fisher picked her and the baby up at the hospital and drove them home.

"AFY provided guidance. Because you were working with the other gangs, besides us, and they were changing, made a difference, too. I am happy that boys from the other gangs are also doing well, just like me. I appreciate that I'm alive and they're alive and able to enjoy life."

To conclude the interview Rey was asked, "What do you believe would have happened in Kalihi in the 1990s if there was no AFY?" He answered, "More people would have been dead or in jail. The gangs would have gone on and on. Honolulu could have been like LA. The work that AFY has done has been awesome. I've seen boys from different groups from the past, but it has never been in a violent way. I saw Roman recently and we hugged each other.

"I don't see the boys from the group much anymore, they've all gone off in different directions. The gang days seem like a different life now."

Cliff

Cliff was born in 1989. His natural grandparents were born in the Philippines, but his father's side goes back four generations in Hawaii and is mixed Filipino and Hawaiian. He considers himself to be more "local" than Filipino. "Local" is a word often used in Hawaii by people of mixed heritage who were born in Hawaii, but it also describes a feeling and attachment to having roots in Hawaii.

He wondered how his father and mother ever got together. They are very different people he said, and their families are very different. His mother's family is more refined. Everybody is real close and mellow. His father's people, on the other hand, he described as roughnecks. He said, "They have no real sense of family. With them it's every man for himself. They get into fights with each other so the family just splits apart. It's kind of mean. People hold grudges. Aunties and uncles don't talk to each other for years, and when they try they just start fighting all over again, so it's pointless. In my dad's family parties always end up in fights."

Cliff said that growing up was pretty tough., He described discipline as harsh. He said that when he was growing up he thought his father was abusive, but looking back be believes it taught him to respect his parents. "Now, when I see the lack of respect that other kids have, I'm proud of the way my dad brought me up," he said. The last time he was thrashed by his father was when he was in tenth grade. The passage of time seems to have dimmed the memory of the times when he said he felt abused and "disciplined a lot." He said that when he was beaten his father would hit him with anything that was handy, including his fists. In the tenth grade he was beaten into unconsciousness. He said, "I came home drunk from a party and I swore at him, and we fought. I thought I could take him because I had already taken down Polynesians who were bigger than me, but I couldn't lay a hand on him and he was only five-foot-six. The next day when I woke up I was tucked into my bed. I thought my mother or grandmother tucked me in, but it turned out it was my father. He apologized to me."

Cliff said that fighting in his father's family was "like a tradition. They all fought. During the 1980s my father was state champion for two years in full-contact fighting."

Cliff said that when his father was his age he was "real bad." "He was a lot worse than what I was. He would go to bars and pick fights when he had nothing better to do." Despite the violence that Cliff experienced and that molded him, he defended his father's behavior as somehow virtuous. He explained, "He never fought anyone smaller than him and would protect the weak. That's what he taught me. I heard from a number of people that he was real humble and never did show off." This description is hard to reconcile with a man who went into bars and picked fights for the heck of it. In an effort to define himself Cliff appears to have created an idealized image of his father. He said, "I really admire him and wish I could be like him." His father works as a security guard. Despite the physical violence that Cliff suffered while growing up he said that he preferred it to the mental torture of his mother's religious lectures.

Cliff's life really started going off the rails when he was in the eighth grade. He started selling marijuana for an uncle, and then began to use drugs himself when he was in the ninth grade. Not only was he selling and using drugs but he also began to steal cars and sell their parts.

He got into the drug business when an uncle asked him if he wanted to make some money. He gave him a pound of pot to sell. It was easy for him and he liked the "adrenaline rush." He said, "I made five grand in less than two weeks. I kept the stuff in my room and nobody in my family caught me. For three years straight that's what I was doing almost every day. I used the money to buy things for my friends. I bought food for the elementary kids who were hungry. I think my parents knew, because I bought things like food and clothes, but they never said anything. Over a three-year period I probably made over $200,000. At the time, drug dealers were few. Nowadays you can find them everywhere—just walking down the street." Cliff's uncle was his supplier during the whole drug-selling period. "I got stopped and handcuffed by the cops a number of times, but they always let me go. I was never actually arrested. The times I was picked up were never for drugs. It was for other things like truancy, fighting, mistaken identity, and for a stabbing where a number of suspects were picked up." It never bothered him that he was breaking the law when he sold drugs. He rationalized that he was giving back to the neighborhood kids who didn't have anything and were "starving." They came from families that were "all broken-up." He said he never expected anything back from the kids for whom he bought food.

Cliff said he had a small group of friends and he would back them up in fights. Although he fought with various gangs he said he never thought of himself as a gang member. He noted that while he backed up his friends he didn't ask them to back him up. He said he liked to fight. "I loved it," he said, emphatically. In the tradition of his father's family he trained in "mixed martial arts."

Despite his denials of gang affiliation, he was in an AFY therapy group, while he was still attending high school, that had members from two clearly identifiable gangs. In twelfth grade, he dropped out of school when his grades fell apart and he joined the National Guard Youth Challenge Program, where he expected to earn his high school diploma. He didn't last a week. "I can't handle taking orders," he said. "It was the same reason that I dropped out of football. Youth Challenge is very controlling and people were telling you what to do all the time."

He said, "I was being put down by the sergeants all the time. At the same time I was being put down by my family. I didn't want to take it anymore. When I decided to leave I met with the commandant who told me some mean stuff. He said that he was told that I was a fighter. 'How can you be a fighter when you don't have the heart to stay here,' he said. I told him, straight out, within these walls you're the man, but out on the street you're nobody. It got to the point that I almost wanted to reach over and yank him across the desk. I guess I got pretty close because the sergeants had to restrain me. They called my dad to come and get me. He was so pissed off that I was grounded for three months.

"My life was pretty messed up. Youth Challenge was supposed to be my last chance. My parents didn't know what to do with me. They told me that I wasn't going to amount to anything and that I was going to end up in prison like one of my cousins. I felt like the people who I looked up to my whole life and who were supposed to love me had turned on me. It was real overwhelming, and I felt so hurt. Now I can understand their frustration and disappointment. The downward spiral began with the drugs. I couldn't focus. I couldn't do anything while I was on drugs. I only did weed but my friends got into cocaine. It frightened me when I saw what it did to them. They just stared out into space and did nothing. They couldn't even watch TV."

Adult Friends for Youth began to work with Cliff when he was in the tenth grade. The process was difficult, with many ups and downs. It was a testament to the Redirectional Therapy principles of "never giving up" and "patience is a virtue."

He was referred to AFY by his school following a huge fight during homecoming week in which two of his friends were hurt and a third was stabbed. He saw his life "crashing," and was desperate to make his family proud of him. Since counseling was being offered, he thought that he would take advantage of it, especially since it was free. Something else was weighing heavy on him. Before his great-grandfather died, he told Cliff that he hoped that he would make something of himself.

Cliff recalled that when he first met Deb and Mo, they asked him to fill out a form that had questions related to drug use (this was not typically something that AFY did, but was a requirement for a drug grant that the agency had acquired). His immediate reaction was "these guys are cops, so I lied about everything." At the second session, when they began talking, the mood of the group began to change. "They didn't judge us and didn't put us down," Cliff said. "My teachers and counselors just told us to drop out already, you're not going to make it.

"Mo and Deb didn't lecture us, they just talked to us. They believed in us when we didn't believe in ourselves. They always kept us feeling up and kept us thinking about what we could do, not about how we had messed up. As I got to know them better, I said to myself, I didn't even know that there were people out there like that."

In the course of the interview, the interviewer said to Cliff, "You said that Mo and Deb were nonjudgmental. We use that term professionally. How is it that you chose to use it?" He responded, "Really simple. When I told them I was doing drugs, selling drugs, stealing cars—you tell an adult that, man, you're in hell, you're a bad kid, what's wrong with you, you're stupid, all that kind of stuff—all they asked was, 'What do you want for yourself?' I never got a lecture. I felt I could just open up and talk. It was like a big, big burden on my chest was dropped. After I met them, that's when I stopped smoking. Nobody had to tell you that it was bad for you. You always understood that anyway. I knew what the facts were. I knew what the consequences were. It was me on my own just doing what felt good at the time. As far as how the group sessions impacted on other members of the group, it was good for some of them, but for others they were so traumatized from growing up that it was real hard for them to open up to someone. For most, the group made them happy. The only time I would go to school was to go to group sessions. We could talk about anything, problems at school, problems with girlfriends, problems at home—it was just good. It was something new for all of us. When we started going to group we had less problems. I really trusted them. They gave me a second chance at life. If it wasn't for them I don't know where I would be, probably in jail or dead.

"Looking back over twenty years of my life I feel I've changed 180 degrees. I graduated high school through AFY's C-Base program. I never thought I would graduate. I was speechless. I was tripping when I graduated. I was overwhelmed. I couldn't even talk straight. There were so many people in the audience supporting us."

Approximately five hundred people attended the graduation for twenty graduates, all of whom were school dropouts. Cliff was one of two commencement speakers. Nearly all of his family was present. After all the lows, this was the high.

"It is a miracle that I'm still here," he said. "Plenty of times I gave up, and even tried to kill myself. I tried three times. The first time I was in ninth grade. My family and I were fighting. I was being put down. I tried to stab myself in the gut, but I couldn't go through with it. The second time was the summer between ninth and tenth grades. It followed the suicide of my calabash cousin on his birthday. About two days before his funeral I was mad at everything. I took my dad's truck out. I didn't have a license or even a permit. It was late at night and everyone was sleeping. Everything hit me while I was driving, so I thought maybe I should just pile up. I was driving back from the North Shore and I tried to fly off the road. I went and wacked the guard rail. Everything flashed and I swear I heard my mother's younger sister, who had died, tell me that it wasn't my time yet. I pulled off the side of the road and was tripping out after I heard that thing in my head. I had to calm down.

"The third time, I tried to hang myself from the plumeria tree in my front yard. I took the dog's chains and tied 'em real tight to the middle of the tree and let myself down real slow. I was hanging and felt like I was there for hours, but it was probably only like six minutes. They say before you die your life flashes before your eyes, but what I saw was only the good stuff, all good memories. I thought, what is happening to me now is because of all the bad choices I made. Then I went all black, and the next thing I knew I found myself on the ground. The chain snapped. I didn't go to school for three or four days because there were like hickies (bruises) all around my neck. After that I said never again. I didn't tell my parents until much later after I was enrolled in AFY's C-Base class.

"After the group started things began to fall into place for me and continued into C-Base. It wasn't like everything changed for the better right away. It was a slow process. Over time things got better. I still had the urge to fight and was just waiting for someone to call me out.

"About one month before graduation I was so happy because my family was happy. It was like when my two younger brothers and I were all kids and innocent. When graduation came my mother was bawling, she was just crying so much. I felt like I was doing it for her and my grandma. Even before the ceremony she was taking pictures and crying. It was my way of saying, 'Sorry. I can't take back what I did,' but I could try to make it up."

Cliff has continued to have counseling sessions with Deb and has brought in cousins who have their own issues. His dream is to one day have his own fighting school, but he says that can wait until he can make honest money and have a family. His immediate plan is to attend community college and learn the refrigeration and air conditioning trade.

When we concluded the interview Cliff had a few more things that he wanted to add. He said, "You guys gave me back my life. I don't know where I would be now if you never came into my life. I know people like me who never had the chance to have you in their life and they're doing real bad. You guys are like angels, I swear to God. You gave me hope. That was the thing I needed most. I didn't have that for a long time. You gave us choices. You didn't force us to do anything. Whatever you are doing with kids, keep it up. It's working. What is it about Deb and Mo that's effective? In bad situations, they don't panic. They go in calm because they aren't thinking about themselves. They care about the youths that they are trying to help."

Trini

Trini was born in Samoa in 1988 and lived half of her life there and half in Hawaii. She moved back and forth, but her adolescent years were spent in Hawaii. Her family is comprised of nine children, five boys and four girls, mother, father, grandmother, and grandfather. One sister continues to live in Samoa.

In Samoa she lived with her grandparents within a traditional highly structured religious village that consisted of twelve extended families. Villages have a curfew and when the bell rings everyone is expected to be home.

Trini said that she likes the freedom of Hawaii but acknowledged that Samoa has less violence. She found herself in what she called the "gang thingee" through her brothers and cousins. She said, "I was always around boys. When my brothers started to get involved I thought it was cool. The boys called themselves the Samoan Gym Rats so when we organized we called ourselves the Samoan Gym Girls. We wanted to be seen as the toughest meanest girls on campus, but it was like a joke. Although most of the school was afraid of us, and we put on this big act in front of everybody, that isn't who we really were. When we were alone we just fooled around like little kids. When we were out in front of the other students it was like, 'You mess with me and I'm going to do something real bad to you.'"

Trini, although she was an integral part of the group, sometimes allowed herself to stand outside of it. She developed the cynical perspective that there was a disconnect between who the girls really were and the bad girls that they wanted everyone else to think they were. She said, "Because I knew them, when they acted big and tough, I just laughed to myself. We all had a need to make other people and ourselves believe we were tough. We didn't smile or show any softness when we were in front of other kids. We just wanted people to believe we were just these hard-knocks, but when we were among ourselves we just wanted to have fun.

"For awhile it was pretty awful. I didn't care about anything. I didn't go to class, or on the rare occasions when I did go I would just cut out. I would meet up with my friends and we would just ditch school. I didn't care about school and I didn't think about the future. I didn't even care if I died. The crew was it. I was willing to risk everything. I lived on the edge. We started fighting a lot. I'd come home late. They whupped and lectured me many times. They were real strict and would even come looking for me, but I stopped caring about what they said or what they did. At one point, I ran away. I'm the kind of person, however, who can't sleep anywhere but my room, so I came back two days later.

"I stayed at my friend's house, but there was no order there. This was another reason for me to quickly end my career as a runaway. Everybody just did what they wanted to do. When I saw that, when they were talking back to their parents, that's when I thought, 'Wow, I do that? Is that the way I talk to my mom? Is that what I do to my dad? I don't like this. I'm going to go back home. I'm going to apologize,' and I did. I decided I didn't want to be a bum. It scared me to be in a home where the kids swore at their parents and threw things at them, and I thought, 'I don't want to end up like this.'

"I also worried about my brothers and sisters turning on my parents and behaving like that. Even though my life was going down the drain I felt I couldn't leave home because I was the one who still had some control over them. When I wasn't going to school I kept my brothers and sisters in school because I didn't want them doing what I was doing."

In response to the question, "How did you feel about yourself at that time?" She replied, "I felt like nothing. I wasn't doing anything for myself. I felt useless. I didn't feel that I mattered. I thought briefly about suicide, but my brother's attempt beat me to it. Then I thought, no way."

The turning point for Trini was a big fight that took place at Keehi Lagoon. "We started it," she said. "The fight involved youth from

Waipahu, Kuhio Park Terrace, and Kam IV. We were all Samoans," she reflected. "I felt not only strange but stupid about it."

When her parents came to the hospital she found out that many of the other kids were related in some way. "Between my parents and the other parents, we were getting lectures from left and right. I told myself, you gotta stop this. It's getting you nowhere."

Her hospitalization gave her time to think, and she came to the conclusion that the "gang thingee" was over for her. "I just couldn't do it anymore," she said.

Her crew kept on going, and put pressure on her, but she stood her ground. They had intentions to jump her out, but her brothers prevented that from happening. As she remembered it, her brothers sent the message that she wanted to graduate and go to college and they understood. She joined the Polynesian Club at school and became its president. She said it kept her going down the right path and away from gang-banging.

Trini became involved with Adult Friends for Youth through her brother, who was in one of McKay Schwenke's groups. Mac started working with her group, separately from the boys, but there was a lot of overlap because the boys and girls hung out with each other. The boys were receiving a huge mount of attention at the time, not from gang-banging, but from public performances of the Haka (Maori dance) and Samoan Slap Dance Mac had taught to them. Among their public performances were the Waipahu May Fair, the AFY Annual Celebration of Youth Fundraiser, attended by over eight hundred people, and a Waipahu High School assembly. They were a big hit wherever they performed.

Trini said that she was in the eleventh grade when she met Mac. "I first thought of him as the 'rugby man,' because he was also teaching the boys rugby and forming them into a team that could compete in AFY's annual rugby tournament. (The tournament has teams from most of the Hawaiian islands, and has had teams from New Zealand, Canada, and Pennsylvania. Both boys' and girls' teams play a fast, seven-a-side game.) Mac helped us realize that there was more to life than trying to be tough. We thought that being a gang member would get us respect, but it was the opposite. It got you nowhere. Without the crew individuals felt lost. They needed the group to feel good about themselves. The group, they believed, gave them prestige. When they were together nobody would challenge them, but when they were by themselves they would get jumped.

"I didn't know Mac but some of the group did. They explained, 'That's Mac, he tries to help out the kids.' I kinda didn't buy it. I said, 'Help out kids? From doing what?' They answered that he has activities that help us do other things from what we usually do.

"I kept my options open, but I noticed how he helped the boys and I noticed how he would talk to us. His being Samoan also helped, but most of all he wasn't like other adults who talked down to us. I felt he understood us. He was down-to-earth. He knows what goes on in Samoan families and why we bring violence to school. Other Samoans would look at you and think bad of you, but he made me feel that he could help me without judging me."

Trini was asked if she could create a model Mac what traits would she give him.

She replied, "I wouldn't want to create a new Mac. I like this one already. He's hilarious. He's down-to-earth. He's just easier to adapt to than anyone else I've tried to adapt to. If everyone else was like Mac this would be a fun world. I've never seen Mac angry. He has a lot of patience. He believes in everybody, and expresses the belief that we could all do better. He never put anyone down. He was somebody I could look up to. I wanted to be like him. He makes people feel good. I want people to feel that way about me. After I met Mac I began to change. I began to care more about school. Before him I never thought about college. After, I began to attend different college meetings. He made me feel confident, real confident."

Trini was a recipient of AFY's Annual Young Person of the Year Award. The year that she received it she was away at community college in Phoenix, Arizona, studying graphic design and animation, so she was not available to receive it in person. She did, however, send a DVD that was played at the fundraiser. Her parents accepted the award on her behalf. Her father was very proud of her and went on a bit, praising AFY for helping her and expressing his thanks. When he told her the story of the evening, he cried. Trini said, "It was the first time I saw him cry from pleasure. It made him feel he had done a good job with me."

"I feel I'm in a good place right now. I've had a few setbacks, but I'm okay. The graphic arts school that I attended lost its accreditation and none of my courses would transfer, so I had to start all over again as a freshman at the University of Hawaii, West Oahu. I was naturally disappointed when it happened. I received an AA degree but now the school only issues a diploma. Nevertheless, I had a great experience in Phoenix. When I was in Arizona I lived off-campus with three other girls. I met kids from Hawaii who are now my friends. They came from communities that we used to fight with. They are now the people who I see most, and I hang out mostly in their neighborhoods. At one time geography, the hood, was what it was all about. Now it doesn't mean anything to me.

"When I was in Arizona I met some Filipino kids who I became friendly with. When they first saw me at Starbucks they said they couldn't believe that the bully of the school was there. They joked, 'Hey, who you trying to beat up?' And 'Who you stealing money from?' I had to say, 'Come on guys, I'm not like that anymore.' "

Trini feels that she has influenced members of her group. When she began to change they also began to change, but she sees very little of them now.

Mac has been her role model. For the positive attitude that she has been able to maintain, even though she had to start all over again at college, and the improved relationship that she developed with her parents where "we really talk with each other," she gives credit to Mac. "He taught me patience," she said.

Her dream is to develop a graphic design and music company. She sees her family being part of the business. She and her brothers sing and play instruments and have performed at church and at schools. She calls her father her partner, who helps her make decisions.

Jenny

Jenny is a wonderful, intelligent, attractive, and engaging thirty-six-year-old woman, who survived a horrible childhood of family disintegration and physical and emotional abuse to emerge as a happily married mother of three children and a very important part of Adult Friends for Youth's leadership team. She wears three separate hats in the organization. She is its fundraising coordinator, director of its annual Student Transition Convention, reaching 9,000 elementary students transitioning to middle school, and administrative assistant to the president and CEO. She was also, as an adolescent, a client of the agency. Like so many of its clients, she is of Filipino descent.

Her parents divorced when she was two years old and her brother was one. Only eleven months separate them. She remembered bouncing back and forth between her mother and father, both of whom had remarried.

The time spent with her mother and stepfather was a nightmare. She remembered crying all the time and not wanting to go back to her mother's place. Her stepfather was a sadist who delighted in torturing the two children. Mother worked at night and Jenny would hide her car keys so she couldn't go to work. When she left the house the beatings and games would begin.

Try as she might to maintain her composure, Jenny cried during the interview, as she recalled the gratuitous violence she endured. She felt it was worse for her than for Chaz because she was a girl. She described what her stepfather did to them as "mind-boggling and abnormal."

They lived on the twentieth floor of a high-rise apartment building. He would lock them in their bedroom so they couldn't use the bathroom. She said she remembered going out on the ledge, twenty floors up, and using it like a bathroom. Her brother held her hand so she wouldn't fall off. When she was out on the edge she thought about "just flying off." She wondered many times, when she was being beaten and abused, "What kind of life is this?" Whenever she thought about suicide she also thought about the consequences for Chaz if she wasn't there for him.

It's interesting to speculate on what someone watching a child going to the bathroom on that ledge might think. "Bad child, we should tell her parents," no doubt. It isn't uncommon where the solution to a child's apparent misbehavior is, "Tell the parents." What a mistake that can be.

One game he played was to have the kids stand by the front door and throw tennis balls at them. If they moved he would hit them with the buckle of his belt. Jenny said some of the neighbors knew something was going on because she talked with some of them. Although she prayed that someone would help them, they never did. If they yelled or screamed he made them eat hot chili peppers or just beat them more.

During one Christmas season he accused her and her brother of taking cookies from a tin of Danish cookies. When they said that they hadn't taken any he made them eat several tins of cookies until they threw up. She was not yet seven at the time.

Jenny's mother refused to listen when Jenny tried to tell her about the horrors she was experiencing. Weekends, although not a paradise either, were decidedly better because they spent them at their father's house. "My father's wife never accepted us, but we were so happy to be there, because at least nobody hurt us. Also, because he lived above my grandmother, we always had cousins to play with. On Sunday I would always cry, because I had to go back and live with my mother, and the week would start all over again."

Jenny recalled never having enough lunch money when she went to school. Her stepfather doled coins out from a cash box. In his convoluted logic, if lunch was forty-five cents and milk was twenty-five cents, then he only had to give them twenty cents for lunch. She said she would go to the office and say that she didn't have enough money for lunch and the school would send home a bill for the additional money. Because she was so fearful of how her stepfather would react, she threw the bill away.

"I was about three or four when my mother married the man, but she had been having an affair with him for some time prior to that," Jenny said. The abuse started from the beginning. There were things that happened, Jenny said, "that I never even told my husband about. My brother doesn't talk about it at all."

Throughout the abuse she suffered, her mother confronted the man only once. It occurred after he placed her hand over a lighter, and her mother asked about the burns.

Her stepfather's parents maintained the YMCA's Camp Erdman and he was a maintenance man at the Central YMCA where the two children attended the Summer Fun Program. He controlled Jenny even there. She remembered that he refused to let her go to the bathroom and she would sometimes urinate in her pants, subjecting her to the ridicule of the other children. She said she was constantly afraid that he was watching her even when she was attending classes. "The YMCA people never suspected his abuse," she said.

"Things improved somewhat when he and my mother had a baby and his attention turned more to the baby. He was happy to have a son. It wasn't long, however, before the two of them began to have problems and she would stay out, fooling around after work, until early in the morning. Then he began to date so we were left to take care of the baby. I was about nine or ten at the time."

While her mother and stepfather were in the process of getting a divorce and the man was dating he was hardly home. Jenny described her feeling as being "so excited" because he wasn't there to hit her. She was ten at the time and her life was about to take another turn.

Jenny remembered that he told them never to open the door for anyone when he wasn't there. Then one day her mother's sisters showed up. "They began knocking on the windows (the family was living in a first-floor apartment at the time) and yelling 'open the door.' We cried back because we were so afraid, 'We don't want to open the door, we don't want to come with you.' They replied, 'Just come with us while he's not here.' We were hiding in our room and they kept pounding on the door and yelling. 'Come on, let's go.'

Finally, we opened the door and they told us to pack our clothes and we just left. I never saw him after that."

After twenty years had passed, she met her half-brother. She was at a shopping mall and saw her mother's sister with a young man. Her aunt asked her if she knew who he was and Jenny replied that she didn't. When her aunt introduced him, Jenny said that all the ugly memories came flooding back. Later Jenny talked with him on the phone and told him that she hated his father because of all the abuse that she had endured. He told her that while he hadn't experienced it, he had heard stories from his half-sisters, after his father remarried, that they also had been physically abused.

In 2008, through a conversation with her half-brother, Jenny learned that his father was dying of cancer. She said she felt no remorse for the abuser who had made her life hell.

After being picked up by her aunts, Jenny and her brother went to live with their maternal grandmother. She said, "Financially it was very hard, because there were other mouths to feed, but at least we weren't being beaten. We did feel abandoned and felt that nobody really wanted us, so we pledged that we would be each other's family. My mom had taken off. I had no idea where she was, and we stopped seeing my real father for over a year because he was busy with his new family. Then one day my grandma said it was time to leave and we should pack up our things because we were going to live with him. She told him, 'These are your kids and you're going to watch them.' We were just dropped off. Still, no one knew where my mother was. Today, she lives in Guam. When she remarried, she didn't tell her new husband that she had children. On a visit to Hawaii, at a family party, she told us to call her auntie. I slipped up and called her mom and that's when he found out that she had children.

"She had me when she was sixteen. Her family called her bad names and told me never to get pregnant like she did. Sure enough, when I was sixteen I became pregnant. I didn't tell my father until I was in my fourth month. The scene was bad. The next day I packed up and went to live with my boyfriend, and never went back. My stepmother didn't want me back and ripped up all my pictures. The family called me a whore in Filipino (Jenny is stilled pained by the memory and cried as she related the story). To this day I see my father only once a year, at Christmas. On one visit he introduced my brother and his other two sons to his friends, but didn't introduce me as his daughter.

"When my children ask about their grandparents I just tell them that we don't get along. They are much closer to my husband's family. When we go to pay our annual Christmas visit they don't interact with the rest of the family. We just sit here and they sit there. I suppose I go with the expectation that maybe one year my father or I might reach out to the other, but it hasn't happened. Even at any age, I still would like to call him 'Dad,' and her 'Mom.' When I had cancer and lost my hair I expected some warmth but it never happened."

Jenny's husband doesn't attend the Christmas visits. He attended a few early on but sees no point in going, and finds the experience excruciating. When her oldest son, now a high school graduate, asked, "Why do we do this every year, it's so fake?" she replied, "I don't know." Actually, she does know. Intellectually, she understands that she has been unable to put the past to rest, and even though she knows it is in vain, keeps hoping for some expression of love. She gave the eulogy at her maternal grandmother's funeral and remembered her mother crying out, "I want my mom back," and thinking, "Oh girl, I wish I had my mom too."

She never had parents to love and nurture her. When she gave birth to her oldest son, the AFY staff member, Terry Fisher, who helped her during her pregnancy, was the only one present at the birth. "I wished she was my mom," Jenny said. Jenny felt neglected and abused throughout her childhood, and always felt unloved and a burden. Terry continued to be a supportive presence in her life well into adulthood. They, subsequently, became colleagues when Jenny joined the staff.

Gang involvement began in middle school. She and her brother were always in the same grade. She said, "He was drawn into the gang life and violence because he was so angry. He got into a lot of fights. I was a loner but Chaz was more sociable. He had lots of friends that he hung out with. School was hard for him because he was one of the youngest students in the class. I helped him with his homework and I also washed his clothes. He slept on the couch at home and when I woke up in the morning he was usually gone."

She remembered that Chaz frequently led gang initiations and that they were violent. She saw boys who were badly beaten. After awhile he stopped attending school and she became frightened for him. Because she didn't know what he was doing and where he was going, she began to hang out with the group just to keep tabs on him. The hangout was at a gym not far from the middle school.

Jenny recalled her first experiences with AFY. "I remember Debbie coming to meet us in a blue van. I was amazed that Chaz actually talked to her about his feelings. He would tell her things that he would never tell me or anyone else. She seemed different and the agency seemed different from other people and organizations that we encountered. We had a lot of respect for AFY and were excited when they came. One thing, they brought food and we were all starving, because we saved our lunch money. When AFY came we knew we were going to have fun and we could talk without being judged as a bad kid. When my brother told me he could trust Debbie, that was an eye-opener for me, because he didn't trust anyone."

Jenny met her boyfriend (later her husband) through his sister. She spent as much time as possible with them because she didn't want to go home. Her girlfriend was going out with Rey, one of her brother's gang friends. Her friend was better off, financially, and had nicer clothes and at first she resented her. Almost twenty years later they remain friends.

Jenny's husband is two years older than she is. He was born and raised in the Philippines. Chaz didn't much like him because he wasn't in the gang.

"When I got pregnant, in the ninth grade, everything changed. I wasn't going home and I wasn't with my brother. I remember one day during my pregnancy, a big fight broke out at Farrington High School and this guy from another gang began to beat up Rey. Without thinking I stood in front of him to protect him and got punched in the stomach. I called Debbie and she came and got me and took me to Tamashiro's Market. I still remember that she bought me pickled mango, and then I went back to school.

"I was never really part of the gang, but, because I was nearly always around them, people saw me as a gang member. The same people who hated the gang also hated me. When people couldn't get to my brother they would come after me instead. But there were also benefits to being Chaz's sister. It gave me power and I used it to get what I wanted. This was the first time I felt in control, because other people wouldn't mess with me. If they didn't listen to me I would threaten to tell my brother. But if you thought you were bigger than the group they would put you in your place. One time, when I was going with a member of the group, he kept me from going to a meeting where my brother was beaten up because he was being too independent and not going along with the group and failing to pay his dues.

"Besides getting into fights, the gang stole cars, but I was never allowed to drive in a car that was stolen. My brother protected me. He always knew where I was and made sure I never went home alone. The fights seemed to be never-ending. I remember my brother and his friend beating up a rival gang member with bats and I was so scared. I thought the guy's friends would come after me.

"Weed was common, but the group tried to keep me from it and also from cigarettes and alcohol, but I did them anyway. I tried it all, including batu (crystal meth), but I didn't like any of them, including the taste of alcohol.

"I had some girl friends, but they were mostly used by my brother and others, but no one was allowed to touch me. Maybe that was why he was so angry when I became pregnant. Sometimes I wonder if Chaz's control over me was a factor in going outside of the group, just to piss him off."

Jenny acknowledged that their relationship became increasingly distant. "We talk but he and my husband are not close. Once I moved out of my father's house I made a choice to accept my husband's family over my own. My choice, at least part of it, was motivated by a need for my child to have a mother and father, unlike the family that I grew up in. We never lived with my husband's parents. We lived with an aunt. I learned to cook, clean, and wash clothes. For the first time I felt I belonged somewhere. She became like a mom to me and helped me when the baby was small. When the baby was born it helped melt the ice with Chaz a little bit."

Jenny said it was hard during the time she was an adolescent to live in Kalihi and not be part of a gang. Friendship groups, she said, tended to be gangs.

"The more you fought and the stronger you were the more popular you became," she reflected. "I didn't feel I belonged, and I wasn't popular until I became identified with Chaz's gang. Once that happened things changed. When I was in ninth grade I was asked to go to the ninth-grade banquet. I was so excited because someone asked me out. He was in my Spanish class, and not a member of our gang. Of course my brother had to approve.

"Over time the group began to change. The boys started to get jobs and became less interested in hanging out. They began to think about better lives for themselves. The group began to move away from the gang life because of AFY. Members wanted to graduate from high school because AFY had pushed them in that direction. In the early days no one thought about graduating. They began to have goals. The boys no longer thought about ending up in prison. Life and the future began to have more meaning. AFY opened their eyes to what they could become. They influenced each other and began to move in the same direction together. It would have been hard if only one had tried to change. This way they supported each other. The support they needed to keep moving forward came persistently from AFY staff. Most of the boys ended up graduating from high school and some went to college. They began to reach for something better.

"In my own life the AFY staff members who most influenced me were Debbie and Terry. They were always there to encourage and nurture me. Their belief in me helped me believe in myself. They helped me get a sense of what I was capable of achieving, and helped me believe that I was a person of value who was entitled to be treated with respect and dignity. They never judged me. I began to believe I could become a happy person."

Chaz continued to be an angry gang-banger for some time, but he too finally began to find peace. After working at a series of menial jobs, he went back to school and learned a trade. He now has a beautiful family of his own and prefers not to talk about the past.

Members of the group still maintain their friendships with each other. Nearly all have separate family lives and get together for occasional birthdays, graduations, and other family events.

Looking back over almost two decades and three children, since the gang days, Jenny says her life is good. She said, "I have the best job in the world. I never believed I would have a career. Even though I don't work directly with the kids, I feel I am making a difference. I see myself in some of the kids and I laugh at some of the things they say. I am actually excited to come to work. How many people can say they love their jobs? This is my family away from my family. My husband and my family are very supportive and also get involved in AFY's programs. They help at the fundraiser and the Student Transition Convention, including traveling to the other islands for the STC. My happiness is very important to my family and to my husband. I feel I want to give back to AFY what everyone gave to me."

As for the future Jenny said, "I want to be at AFY until the day I die, or at least until I retire." She concluded, "If AFY had not come into my life I believe I would have been a very abusive person. I would have been abusive to my kids, and my husband and I wouldn't have been together. I would have just continued the cycle that I experienced."

Chapter 7

Four Adolescent Gangs

Chapter six shared stories of twelve young friends out of the hundreds that Adult Friends for Youth has reached in over two decades of practice. Most of the help that AFY has provided took place within the context of their natural friendship groups/gangs. A taste of what practice looks like within the group will be presented in this chapter.

BABY HAWAII BROTHERS

Kalihi Filipino Youth Club (name changed when the group evolved from a gang into a club).

Staff Member: Deborah L.K. Spencer-Chun, MSW

The Baby Hawaii Brothers (BHB) took their name from the older, infamous Hawaii Brothers. They were engaged in a range of antisocial/criminal behaviors, from truancy to fighting, assault, terroristic threatening, auto theft, and graffiti.

I first met the boys while on a picnic with another group of Farrington High School students. Bart Evans, a second-year MSW practicum student, had gone to obtain food for the boys and asked if another worker and I would monitor them. While he was gone the members got into some trouble with the police and I intervened. Apparently, when the guys were left alone, they had gathered on a huge boulder, and, upon observing an officer in a scooter pass by, began making siren noises and jokes. This triggered a trouble call. Before long, eight officers arrived on the scene. At first, because I was cooking, I was unaware of all that was happening. A member of my group finally called my attention to the situation. I immediately went over to check on things. When I arrived I found some of the boys being searched while the others sat on the ground with the police standing over them. I asked what was going on and was yelled at by a police officer, who obviously had no idea that I was a social worker (I'm sure I looked like one of the kids). He wanted to know what business it was of mine. I explained my position and again asked him what was going on. My professional role made no impression on him, and I was nastily told, "If you're their social worker, why the hell aren't you watching them?" I turned to another police officer who politely responded to me and explained the details. When I later approached the officer who yelled at me, he apologized. I again explained who I was and about the agency. I told them that I did not think the boys meant any harm and asked that they be left in my care. The officers softened and, after giving their obligatory lecture to the boys, left the scene.

My ability to advocate successfully was not lost on the group, and it raised their curiosity about me and my job. I explained what our agency did and suggested that we might be able to help them with school (homework, advocating on their behalf with school staff, and tutoring), home (getting along with brothers and sisters, parents, and other family members), community (fights with other gangs), legal system (police, probation officers, and upcoming court dates), and finding jobs. I said that as a friend I could help them with issues that were of concern to them, and that, just as important, we could do lots of things that were just fun.

The boys listened patiently and eventually vented their feelings about their relationship with the police. They felt that the police were rough on them, and harassed them too often. I provided the opportunity for them to express these feelings without being scolded or lectured to. This helped them feel that someone cared enough to listen to their concerns and helped them relax. It advanced our relationship. We later played cards and they taught me how to play a game called pipito. They seemed excited to have been able to teach me this game.

Throughout the forming stage of group intervention (we call it the seductive phase), we did fun things with the group to help them get to know us, as well as for us to know them. I always allowed them the opportunity to talk to me about anything without judging them. I also allowed the members to decide on activities so that there was never any doubt that the group belonged to them and that they had a say in things.

I usually visited the group in school and on their turf a couple of days a week, even on non-meeting days, to see how they were doing. This gave them the opportunity to ask questions or talk about things that came up outside of group sessions.

Early on, I explained the ethics of confidentiality and treated them with respect. I looked beyond their antisocial behaviors and got to know them as people, not just gang members. I accepted them for who they were and they appreciated that. In fact, there were many times when I forgot they were members of a gang and simply thought of them as kids with issues that are common to all adolescents.

My style is relaxed, but firm, which means that I am able to relate to the guys and joke with them about almost anything. I often provide them with opportunities to talk to me by asking questions, but I am careful not to make them feel that I am being pushy.

I often express my concerns and feelings for them and from time to time raise questions about their safety. I also express to them that my job does not stop once I drop them off, but that I care about them and often think of them and worry about them. I attempt to relate to them empathically by understanding their reason for behaving as they do, just as I would like people to relate to me without first judging me (this seems to be the Golden Rule of Redirectional Therapy). I am honest about what I do on their behalf. For example, if I speak with a school counselor, I explain what the discussion was about so that they aren't surprised later. I encourage them to be open and honest with me, and I try to be open and honest with them. We also give and receive feedback from each other. This is what the agency meant when it established the philosophical principle that emphasized mutual and respectful relationships as essential to an effective therapeutic relationship.

I attempt to be sensitive to them and to empathize with what they are going through. I often advocate for them in areas where they feel helpless. Yet, I try to improve their coping skills so that they can advocate for themselves. For example, when one member felt that he couldn't talk to anyone about a teacher who he felt hadn't been treating him fairly in class, I listened to him and asked how he would like me to help. I then encouraged him to meet with his counselor. If students feel uncomfortable doing this alone, I will go with them. After the initial visit with the counselor, I find that they usually feel safe enough to follow up on their own. Once they learn how to initiate a meeting, they feel empowered and not so helpless.

Another example of advocacy occurred when I advocated on their behalf regarding allegations that they were mistreated by some policemen. In this case, I, other staff members, and the boys met to address the issue of the misconduct with superior officers of the policemen. We confronted the issues together. The knowledge that adults were on their side and that they weren't alone enabled them to openly express their side of the story and how they felt about the issue of abuse of power by the police.

The boys know that I am fair. Although I will advocate on their behalf, they know that I will also confront them if they have done something that is not in the best interests of the group, are jeopardizing themselves, or pose a threat to another group member. I will express my disappointment, when warranted, by stating how I honestly feel about an act or statement. When the members establish rules for the group, they often expect guidance from me to see that the rules are honored. At the same time, they know that they have an obligation to themselves, as well as to the group, to do the same. For example, if a member has broken a group rule, they know that if I am aware of it I will call them on their inappropriate behavior. They also know that it is their responsibility to help their fellow members understand the wrong and provide a means to correct it.

I explore alternative behaviors with them through discussion and by just allowing them to behave as themselves. Often they are criticized for normal teen-aged behavior by adults who expect them to behave the way they want them to behave. In the group I allow them to be themselves and give them a chance to feel good about who they are as people.

I start where they are as individuals and where they are as a group. I do not judge them but provide opportunities for them to discuss issues. Each member of the group has his own issues and concerns but as a group they may have other shared problems. For example, an individual member may be dealing with a fight he's had with his parents the night before, but the group as a whole has the problem of parents not understanding them as adolescents. In this case, the issue is both individual and group and must be addressed at two different levels.

Problem Solving

I try to teach them skills so that they can solve problems as they arise. One such skill is brainstorming, during which they are encouraged to identify concerns and present alternative solutions. For example, we have brainstormed and then discussed alternatives on how they can deal with rival gang issues. We have also discussed what would be the consequences for each alternative. Sometimes, these discussions are informal and take place in the van on the way to or from an activity.

The Six-Point Plan

I have discussed all the areas of this plan with the group and have provided them with the opportunity to brainstorm about activities they would like to do. We try to rotate our activities around their suggestions in the six areas. For example, one week we may decide to do something from the area of sports and recreation. In one such activity the group played basketball against the staff. This was fun and provided intimacy. They enjoyed the closeness even though they lost. We gathered for a snack with the staff afterward, and, thus, enhanced the sociability of the event. In the area of education, we have visited the University of Hawaii campus, discussed the academic process for continuing education after high school, and provided the opportunity to think about future career plans.

Food

Food opens the door for relaxation and helps members feel valued. Since it is hard to talk on a hungry stomach, it also enhances discussion.

Food also helps to reduce barriers and tensions that are present during the forming stage. I remember, after one gang fight, the boys were still very tense and food curbed not only their hunger but also calmed their anger and enabled them to talk more reasonably.

Other Services

- Helping members look for a job.
- Advocating for group members.

- Meeting with parents when appropriate and necessary for their well-being.
- Meeting with neighboring systems, e.g., teachers, counselors, and police officers.

The service we provide is on the group's turf. In the case of the BHBs, it is a nonpublic Kalihi apartment complex. This is where I pick up the boys for their outings and is the place where we sometimes hold meetings or just "talk story." Almost all of the boys either live in these apartments or within a three-to-four block radius.

Established Guidelines

The rules that the group established were followed by everyone, including me. For example, the group established the rule that for any curse word used by members, they pay a quarter. Once we went hiking and a couple of the boys hid in the bushes with the intent to scare me. They succeeded completely and I accidentally blurted out a word. The group instantly fined me a quarter.

Education

Education is an important factor in the process of change. Although there is a myth that gang members do not care about school, I found that for this group it was simply not true. The boys were very concerned about their educations, and one day, on an outing, they asked about possible tutoring. They felt they needed to put aside time to study and needed someone to help them. We discussed their concerns and negotiated arrangements. The final outcome was that the group would study every day after school for as long as it took if I provided transportation from school to the office and then home. I agreed, with the result that tutoring took place for the entire school year. The attendance and participation for the first two quarters (one semester) was large and consistent. The last two quarters' participation was smaller but still very consistent for those that attended.

Problems Encountered

Unlike other therapeutic groups that are time-limited and have fixed memberships, this is an open group in which some transiency occurs. These comings and goings sometimes present problems. Tino, who was committed to the Youth Correction Facility for two years, presented an example of just such a problem when he was released. Unaware of the changes the group had made, Tino tried to get them back into antisocial behaviors. Out of fear and loyalty, the group was caught in a dilemma. Fortunately, after much soul-searching, the group stood its ground. I have since engaged in many informal conversations with Tino to help him understand the group's progress during his absence.

Another member, Ken, also attempted to pressure the group into fighting and illegal activities by accusing members of disloyalty. In fact, during a lengthy discussion, the group talked about how they "loved" Ken, and about his always being there for them when they needed him. Finally, after thinking deeply about the problem, they concluded that instead of going backward they needed to help him reach their level, and that if he cared about them he wouldn't expect them to slip back to where they used to be. This decision to cut themselves free was very painful.

Police harassment has generated much anger. Even though they've changed, they feel that police attitudes have remained the same. They now want the same protection from the police that other law-abiding citizens receive, but instead they have found their civil rights grossly violated. After one particularly brutal incident, in which a group riding in a car was stopped and malevolently abused on the freeway, including being picked up by their belts and collars and dropped face first onto the roadway, AFY responded by holding several meetings with Honolulu Police Department personnel, including an Assistant Chief of Police. The incident was initiated by a motorist who thought he saw a gun through the car's rear window. He called the police on his cellular phone to report it. The "gun" turned out to be a hair brush.

Subsequently, some of the members also participated in a presentation to a police class to share their views. This provided an opportunity for the police to understand the boys' point of view and to get to know them as human beings. Group members have overcome many of their problems and have proved that they are worthy of the community's trust. They continue to educate the community as a whole by attending meetings and giving presentations.

Over time the group evolved from a gang to a social club of friends. Indicative of their new status was the decision to change their name to the Kalihi Filipino Youth Club (KFYC).

Goals of the Kalihi Filipino Youth Club (Baby Hawaii Brothers)

As the members of the KFYC found themselves becoming increasingly successful in school, and as graduation loomed more realistically, they began to talk more about what they expected out of life. In summary, their goals were to:

1. Graduate
2. Continue to provide the community with insight on adolescent gangs
3. Be able to function in the mainstream
4. Go to college and further their education
5. Work at satisfying jobs

The goal "to graduate" reminded me of a discussion with one of AFY's female gangs. Most of the members were in the eleventh grade at the time, and all said they expected to "grad." They had come to AFY's attention in the ninth grade because of their chronic truancy and fearsome reputation. When asked during the discussion if graduation was also their goal back then, they replied in near unison: "No, because we didn't think we would live long enough."

Basically, the KFYC is now on a maintenance program. I occasionally meet with them as a group, but we mostly work on individual issues as they arise. When I first met with them, they got into fights on a weekly basis. Many members had police records and did not see school as an important factor in their lives. Family Court and probation officers were a norm, and family relations were poor. During three years of work, I saw the group go through many ups and downs, but in the end, they succeeded as successful human beings, each in his own way.

A member of another gang stated that he felt this group was being "good guys" and did not make any more trouble. They developed a positive reputation in the community and were quite pleased with their new reputation. They still had a "rep" but of a different kind.

JUNIOR SONS OF SAMOA (JR. SOS)

Staff Member, Pasimi Hingano, PhD

The Junior Sons of Samoa was the third youth gang out of six generations of the SOS gang that resided in Kuhio Park Terrace (KPT), a low-income housing project located in the Kalihi community of Honolulu. The Jr. SOS had a membership of twenty-two and was organized by their "godfather," who was a member of the older generation, Hard Core. Even though the godfather seldom hung out with the juniors, the important decisions of the gang were finalized by him. In the absence of the godfather there was no designated leader. Activities, however, were mostly determined by a core of six members. Prior to intervention their criminal activities were mainly truancy, shoplifting, fighting, auto theft, burglary, and assault. I applied Redirectional Therapy (RT) in three phases; (1) rapport establishment, (2) behavioral change, and (3) maintenance.

Establishing rapport was critical, because without it the other two phases would obviously never have occurred. The development of a trusting relationship allowed gang members to be comfortable and receptive in their interaction with me. Some of the principles I utilized in the phase were: (1) genuine expressions of care and interest in helping them, (2) exhibiting a nonjudgmental and noncondescending attitude, and (3) recognition of their potential to change.

At our very first activity, a picnic at Sand Island Beach Park, we sat around a picnic table eating chili with rice. After we finished, I sensed that I had their attention to express how I felt about them and to explore their expectations of me. I thanked them for inviting me into their group as one of their friends, and said, "I use the word friend because I wish that you will treat me as a friend rather than just a social worker. I want to help you, but I cannot do it alone. I need your help. . . how can I help you?" There was silence for a minute or two, as they looked down and played with their fingers.

Finally, Jimmy replied, "I don't know, man, we are fucked up already." They laughed, and then Lorenzo said, "Maybe keep us out of trouble. . . if you can."

After that day I spent countless hours just "hanging" with them at school during recess and lunch, and at KPT after school. When members were absent from school, I showed up at their homes just to check if they were all right.

When I began hanging with them, they had certain behaviors that seemed so "uncivilized and barbaric," such as spitting anywhere they walked or sat, eating like animals, and using vulgar and profane language. I communicated to them that those behaviors were, in the eyes of many people, socially unacceptable, and that sometimes I, too, felt uncomfortable.

During the times I spent with them, I adapted to and absorbed their socialization style as if I were another member, while still maintaining my professional position. I was able to maintain this dual role by always being conscious of what I was doing and why I was doing it.

At Sand Island, during one activity, we played horseback fight in the water. I rode their backs and they rode on mine. This seemingly childish game allowed me to further cement our relationship. At other times, we simply shared jokes and stories. As activities and time passed, they accepted me more and more.

From the first meeting, I expressed my strong conviction that I believed they were capable of changing their antisocial behaviors and adopting positive ones. I continued to emphasize my belief in their ability to change, especially when illegal and/or destructive acts occurred.

On one occasion, we sat around the basketball court in KPT while they expressed how much they disliked school, and that all they wanted to do was "party." I explored why they felt that way. Mike mentioned that he felt their teachers thought they were stupid. I asked, "Do you believe that?" A few of them just grumbled, "Fuck them, we ain't stupid."

I agreed that they weren't stupid and emphasized my belief that they could graduate if they wanted to. That evening they each shook my hand, before they left, and thanked me for believing in them.

Behavioral Change

Redirectional Therapy believes that members of youth gangs are open to the experiences provided by the education, work, athletics, community service, social, and cultural activities, which make up of the Six-Point Activity Plan, but that they are just so far out of touch with many of these experiences that they feel lost, with no direction. This is where therapeutic guidance becomes useful. A discussion of the therapeutic intervention process follows.

Education

After our fourth meeting it became obvious that these boys always dreamed of "walking the line" on graduation day. I asked the question, "Do you want to graduate from Farrington?" They raised their voices in unison and said, "Hell yeah!"

Jimmy then asked the question, "But how can we? It's too late, Simi, we are fucked up already." This seemed to be a common response for him, reflective of the hopelessness that he felt.

After we explored their reasons for assuming it was too late, it became clear that the problems were truancy, which was further complicated by drinking, almost on a daily basis; too many suspensions from school because of fighting; bad grades because they did no homework; and the feelings of helplessness because most were already one or two grades behind.

Our discussion focused on kindling the hope that graduation was still possible if they would commit to working on it or at least to giving it a try. Immediately, questions from the serious to the ridiculous were thrown at me. Probably out of disbelief, Jimmy assertively asked, "So what, Simi, are you gonna get me out of bed every morning to go to school?" then he laughed. "Can you talk to my English teacher? She is an asshole," Sam chimed in. Lorenzo jokingly commented, "Simi, Mike is an alcoholic already . . . he is no hope."

Even though there was a little reluctance on their part to make a commitment, it was strongly implied that they wanted to graduate and also needed help with a variety of problems. I was relieved to know that they wanted assistance and would welcome help from me.

As I became increasingly involved, I learned more and more about each member's problems, so, while using the context of the group to process and reinforce their development, I also started to work with them on an individual basis. These are some of the things I did with them individually:

1. I explored, with their school counselors, the problems and important steps necessary for success in their respective classes. For example, Counselor S. informed me that Jimmy needed to wear his P.E. uniform during P.E. class, or he was going to fail. Counselor B. reported that Sam and Lorenzo needed to take summer classes to complete their tenth-grade requirements.
2. I conferred with teachers with whom the boys indicated they had difficult relationships. Mr. D. reported that Horse, Jimmy, and Mike had many absences and, even when they went to class, usually didn't do any work. Mrs. A. informed me that Paul swore at her on many occasions, and, consequently, she made him stand in the corner of the room.

I then met with the boys individually and discussed these concerns. They expressed interest in conforming and making a full commitment. Nevertheless, I followed up on them almost daily and the results were as follows:

Jimmy's mother sewed him a uniform that could cover his obesity, and Jimmy started wearing it for P.E. class. Lorenzo and Sam registered for summer classes and worked hard the whole summer in school.

Since drinking alcohol was a problem for Mike and Jimmy, as well as the others, they proposed to make an effort to quit. When school started in September, they informed me that they only drank on weekends. This helped their attendance to improve and greatly reduced their tardiness.

Their progress in school, as well as other areas of their lives, was recognized and verbally rewarded during our weekly group meetings. This reinforcement helped to encourage them and keep them motivated.

Community Projects

The Jr. SOS participated in numerous projects, including singing Christmas carols and distributing gifts and refreshments to the elderly at the Hale Nani Nursing Home, and removing graffiti at Dot's Grocery Store. These projects resulted from group decisions to do something productive for their community.

The elderly patients at Hale Nani were delighted with the performances and pleased with the attention they received from the boys. Some of the patients were overcome by emotion and their eyes filled with tears. The experience also had a profound impact on the boys. On the way home in the van, they spoke almost reverently about how the old people reminded them of their grandparents and how happy they had been.

The graffiti they removed from Dot's Store was graffiti that they had put there. It had covered the store's walls for years. It has now been several years since this painting project, and still there is not a single letter or any other type of graffiti written on those walls. They took ownership of this positive work and developed an increased sense of community responsibility.

Recreation

Recreation activities were an important part of the behavior process, not only to keep the boys occupied, but to motivate, reward, and teach good sportsmanship and other socially appropriate behaviors. They also cultivated receptive "hearts" to the exploration and discussion of solutions to other problems.

The Jr. SOS always looked forward to going to special activities, such as movies, picnics, and football games. At the end of every activity they thanked me for taking them. At times their behaviors were boisterous but not uncontrollable.

The first time we went to a movie theater, they were loud and obnoxious, and the ushers warned them to quiet down. After the movie, when we were in the van, relaxed, happy, and ready to go home, I felt that they would be receptive to a brief processing of their behaviors and a discussion of consequences if such behaviors persisted in the future. They apologized for what they had done and then asked how they could be punished. I explained that the consequences could be the loss of free movie passes from the theater company and denial of access to this particular theater. The problem never occurred again.

Maintenance

Two years after I began, eleven Juniors had graduated from high school and by September, seven of them were attending community colleges. A few dropped out, either because they were seventeen or eighteen years old and still in grade nine, or because their families needed them to work for financial reasons. By the following year, every single member was either working or going to school. The graduation rate went from 10 percent at the time I began to approximately 80 percent, five years later. The arrest rate dropped significantly—during the fourth and fifth years I was not in court for any Jr. SOS member. Subsequently, I was able to place the Juniors on maintenance status, where we met only once a month. However, there were no restrictions on making individual or group contact with me should the need arise. They moved on and the type of call that I received, subsequently, was to invite me to a birthday party, or other family event, and, sometimes, to help in obtaining employment or securing a driver's license. In the old days they were never occupied with getting jobs, and driving without a license was never of concern either.

FLIPSIDE PINOY

Kalihi Youth Club
Staff Member: Rick Bunney, MSW

I was introduced to a member of the Flipside Pinoy Boys, Carl, through a colleague who conducted a school group with him at Farrington High School. Carl's cousin was a member of the Baby Hawaii Brothers, another Filipino youth gang that was, at the time, also receiving services from AFY. Carl stated that his gang was interested in receiving some help too, so I offered to be their social worker if they wanted me. Carl introduced me to his friends and I, subsequently, began running a summer group with them. The summer was spent building trust and rapport. In the year that followed, the group began to shift away from being a "gang" and toward becoming a "youth club."

This case study begins with an overview of the group's behavioral profile before and at the time of intervention by AFY. The group is referred to by its club name, the Kalihi Youth Club (KYC).

"Flipside," as they were called on the street, engaged in numerous antisocial behaviors, before and at the time of intervention by AFY. Among them were poor academic performance, truancy, tardiness, and disruptive behavior in the classroom. Criminal behaviors ran the spectrum from status offenses to misdemeanors to felony charges. Among these were curfew violations, running away from home, petty theft, trespassing, grand theft auto, and terroristic threatening. Although not arrested for illicit drugs, the gang engaged in smoking marijuana, crack, and ice, as well as the consumption of alcohol. The gang was not, however, involved in the distribution or trafficking of these drugs.

Our initial group sessions were held at the beach, where we swam, relaxed, and ate lunch together. AFY supplied the food as well as the transportation. My personal style built the foundation for long-term services.

In the forming stage, I believe it is important to be a positive "Adult Friend." My goal was to convey unconditional positive regard to each member, so that he could feel accepted for whom he was, without strings attached. When a youth feels respected, a relationship based on mutual trust and genuine concern can begin to build. I believe I was successful in conveying this feeling of acceptance at the onset of my work with this group.

After the second group outing, the boys began to ask for my assistance in helping them obtain summer employment. I accompanied them to potential employers to acquire applications and help them complete the forms. For example, Carl and "T" did not know what "references" meant, and I was able to not only explain the concept but let them know that when I got to know them better, they could also use me as a reference. In fact, a few months later, Carl did use me as a reference for a couple of jobs, and I was able to recommend him confidently. I was also able to take the boys to their job interviews and process their anxieties and concerns about the experience with them.

Another way I built trust with the group was to be honest and "up front" from the beginning. I made it clear that I was not in their lives to tell them what to do, nor would I attempt to tell them how they should live their lives. I explained that my role was to help and support them and not to be an informer for the police, nor to take the side of their parents. Through my work, I demonstrated that I meant what I said.

I identified five problems as common to either some or all of the members of the KYC:

1. LOW SELF-ESTEEM. At a time when teenagers are struggling to determine who they are and what they want out of life, experiencing low self-esteem is not uncommon. Given the life circumstances of the high-risk youth I work with, the cycle of poverty, belonging to an ethic minority, and being an immigrant, serve to compound feelings of unworthiness. In fact, low self-esteem appears to be the underlying problem related to many of the other problems exhibited by these boys. I have observed the following statements and behaviors that reveal the low opinion that most of the kids have of themselves.

a. Self-defeating statements:

- I can't go to college. I'm not smart enough.
- I can't do it.
- I'm not good enough.

b. Questioning why AFY works with gangs:

Several members of KYC have asked me why AFY bothers to work with kids in gangs. The underlying message appears to be, "We're losers, so why waste your time trying to help us?" My response is, "I really care about you. I love you guys, and if I can help you to have fun and to begin thinking about what you want to do with your lives and maybe work through some problems in order to get there, then AFY and I will have served a good purpose."

c. Intimidation about job interviews:

Virtually all of the boys expressed concern over participating in the job interview. Aside from the normal anxieties that accompany inexperience, minority kids express fear over not being able to speak proper English. English, to some, is their second language, and the local dialect, or pidgin, is structured and pronounced differently. This all combines to intimidate them and has a marked effect on the way they feel about themselves.

2. FEAR. Endemic to gang membership are enemies. It is the ultimate definition of "we-ness" and "they-ness." When one dons a colored rag, he not only has instant friends but has instant rivals as well. As a result, fear becomes an everyday fact of life that influences the simplest activities of daily living. For example, walking down the street is an exercise in logistics, to be undertaken only in a group or, if you are alone, by packing a weapon. This type of insecurity also manifests itself in the form of posturing, or walking or acting "bad" in order to prove to others that "I am not afraid—I'm bad." Kalihi has its "safe" zones and "danger" zones. Carl has a long history of conflict in

various neighborhoods and had "friends" and "enemies" scattered throughout. Simply walking down the street brings with it different levels of fear. Carl prefers to walk with one or more of his friends, or he "watches his back" if he walks alone. When he perceives possible danger his posture becomes more rigid and he becomes emotionally tense and guarded.

3. LACK OF SOCIAL SKILLS. Limited proficiency with the English language inhibits many local youth from opportunities in mainstream society. Although most of the kids I work with want jobs, they do not actively seek employment. The interviewing process intimidates the hell out of them (How do I act? What do I say? What do I wear?). And when they do obtain employment, it usually doesn't involve public contact.
4. PROBLEMS WITH ANGER MANAGEMENT. Inappropriate role models, experience with domestic abuse, a sense of powerlessness, and low self-esteem combine to create few positive modes for expressing one's anger. Communicating in a hostile world does not seem possible, and the result is dysfunctional peer, family, and interpersonal relationships. The Redirectionalist is nondirective. Views are expressed authentically by giving "I" messages. The CA doesn't give advice by pronouncing what the adolescent should or shouldn't do but helps the adolescent assess the situation and work out solutions that s/he believes are in her/his best interests.

Carl was involved in an argument with his mother that resulted in his hitting her and knocking her to the ground, injuring her back and shoulder. When I spoke with him the day after the incident, he was concerned about his possible arrest:

Carl: Man, the cops is after me.
Rick: How come?
Carl: 'Cause I went knock down my muddah.
Rick: You hit her?
Carl: Yeah—she fuck'n went call Tammy one whore.

Rick: Hmm. Did your mom call the cops?
Carl: No. My uncle—them did.
Rick: They saw it happen?
Carl: No. They heard it.
Rick: What did you do?
Carl: I took off. I went bag.
Rick: (Pause) What are you going to do?
Carl: I'm not going home, that's for sure.
Rick: You're not going home—where do you plan to sleep?
Carl: Tammy's.

Later that day I spoke to Carl's mother on the telephone. She told the police that she had fallen in the pantry so that they wouldn't arrest her son. My next conversation with Carl dealt with his feelings about the incident with his mother and how he thought his mother felt about it:

Carl: I been sneaking into the house at night.
Rick: To sleep?
Carl: No. To get clothes and food.
Rick: Does your mom hear you?
Carl: I think so but she never say nothing.
Rick: You're not talking to each other?
Carl: Nope.
Rick: How come?
Carl: I don't know, 'cause she mad I think.
Rick: Why do you think she's mad?
Carl: 'Cause I went knock her down and make her bang her da kine, shoulder.
Rick: Do you want to talk about that?
Carl: About what?
Rick: Hurting your mom.
Carl: (silence)
Rick: (Pause) How do you feel?
Carl: (Long Pause) Shame. I feel shame.

The next day I asked Carl if he had spoken to his mother. He said, "No," and, responding to my curious probing stated, "Yeah Rick, I going for apologize. It just never happen yet." It took another day, but Carl apologized to his mother. Without giving advice on what he should or should not do, I told him I was concerned for him, and I helped him process the situation in terms of his feelings and understanding of the problem. Through this he was able to talk the situation out and arrive at a solution that was in his (and his mother's) best interest.

5. LACK OF SOCIAL RESPONSIBILITY. What society deems responsible behavior (attending school, obtaining employment, and becoming a productive member of society) was not part of the behavioral repertoire for most of these youth. Nevertheless, this is not to say that they are incapable of achieving and succeeding. Instead, their needs and life circumstances are different than most middle-class teenagers. Violations of the law are interpreted as a lack of social responsibility in the dominant culture, but are normative in what Sutherland and Cressey (1955) referred to as the differentially associated culture. The KYC certainly had their share of brushes with the law.

A year prior to intervention by AFY, Carl and a few other Flipside Pinoys were involved in a serious confrontation with the police. They stole a car and were cruising around in it when the police spotted them. In an attempt to arrest them, a car chase ensued. The police managed to stop them, but in the process, both cars were damaged and an officer was threatened with a knife. Carl was charged with grand theft auto, interfering with official acts, and terroristic threatening, among other things. Although he was sixteen years old at the time, his juvenile case was waived over to adult court. Going before the judge and coming face to face with a future in prison served to change his attitude dramatically. He stated that he no longer wanted to be involved with "gang stuffs," and he wanted to straighten out his life. Fortunately, AFY had the opportunity to intercede shortly thereafter, and was able to support him in his effort to become the productive person that he wanted to be.

Methods of Building Rapport

Four effective methods of building rapport with the KYC were implemented involving physical activities, the use of food, verbal communication, and personal style.

1. PHYSICAL ACTIVITIES. Engaging in activities that were interesting to the KYC created bonding as they shared common experiences. Activities included swimming, playing basketball, cruising, going to the movies, and conducting car washes.
2. THE USE OF FOOD. "Breaking bread" has probably been a means for developing and maintaining relationships since the beginning of human history. It is gratifying and soothing, and breaks down barriers. Food, in one form or another, has been present at every group session. Sometimes it is as elaborate as a picnic or going to a restaurant, and, at other times, as simple as passing around a bag of chips and sodas or sharing candy bars.
3. VERBAL COMMUNICATION. Providing an opportunity for the kids to learn, through education, explaining concepts, and discussing issues and problems important in their lives, is an excellent method of establishing rapport. Also, by just "talking story" (small talk), the boys found new insights into their problems and ways of resolving them.
4. PERSONAL STYLE. I would describe my basic therapeutic style as "approachable" or "down to earth." I am open and honest with the kids and am able to express my feelings in a genuine manner to which, I believe, high-risk kids, who seldom have positive adult role models in their lives, can relate. I believe that by not being preachy and not playing the Fairy Godmother or Godfather, who has all the answers and can solve all the

problems, I have been able to establish myself as just another human being who has strengths that can be learned from, but who has his own vulnerabilities as well. I may have my own views, which I feel free to share, but that doesn't mean that I expect others to accept them. The boys know that when I talk about what has been good for me, it doesn't mean that I believe it will be good for them, but at the same time it doesn't mean it wouldn't be good. What it does mean is that I'm sharing something from me that I hope they will think about. By showing concern for the well-being of the boys, I established myself as "helper" or "change agent." Once they felt comfortable with me as a person who was interested in helping them, they began to seek my help. An example of this is demonstrated in the case of Erwin, who initially kept his distance from me. When I first met him he was quiet and somewhat aloof. He spoke to me only when I initiated the conversation, and even then communication was stilted. Over time he became more comfortable with me, and, as his comfort level grew, he started to initiate contact. Communication proceeded from, "Howzit, Rick?" to asking for help in getting a job.

Implementation and Outcomes of Redirectional Therapy

Over time the person-centered, nonjudgmental approach of Redirectional Therapy resulted in a marked increase in responsible behavior by Carl. He moved from very dangerous criminal behaviors, that had him marked for prison and/or death by violence, toward more constructive prosocial behaviors.

By the time Carl was seventeen, he had been involved in youth gangs for five years. He had numerous criminal violations and was more involved in drugs than any other member of the group. Underneath it all, however, he was frightened and was motivated to improve his life. He was unaware of how to effectively search for employment, so I taught him how to read the classified ads and obtain applications that could lead to a job. I transported him to job interviews and counseled him on effective interviewing skills. I also served as a reference for him on job applications. I assisted him in obtaining a driver's license by providing an automobile for the road test, and I helped him practice for the exam. I supplemented his basic driving skills by teaching him parallel parking, the appropriate use of mirrors, and signaling. Regular group outings provided an opportunity for Carl and his girlfriend to spend quality time together and to engage in activities that were new, stimulating, and outside of the neighborhood.

The agency and I were also there for him when his girlfriend went into labor. My supervisor transported her to the hospital and assisted her with the admissions process while I looked for Carl at school. We provided support for both of them at a time when neither had support from their families. I also accompanied them into the delivery room and was present when she had her baby.

On another occasion, I was able to offer support after one of Carl's best friends was murdered. He and other group members served as pallbearers at the funeral. I was able to help the kids acquire T-shirts in memory of their slain friend, accompany them to the wake, and provide transportation to the funeral. It was an emotionally charged experience due to the circumstances of the death at the hands of drug dealers, the fact that the boy had been a long-time friend, and that the funeral was held on the birthday of one of the pallbearers.

I organized a birthday picnic following the funeral, which allowed the group time to mourn and process their feelings in a safe environment.

The CA Communicates Care and Love for Group Members

A caring relationship developed between Carl and myself, the extent of which even I was unaware until an incident occurred that brought tears to my eyes. During a group session, we were getting into the van and a fistfight broke out between Carl and his girlfriend. I intervened so that neither party would get physically hurt. In an attempt to do this, I grabbed both of Carl's wrists to stop his punching, while I told another group member to hold Tammy. Immobilized, Carl directed his anger at me and tried to punch me. Surprised, and at a loss for what to do, we exchanged a few moments of eye contact and then I said, "I don't know what to do, Carl." His anger and frustration turned to tears as he gave up the fight and sank back in his seat. Upset over the fact that Carl became so angry that he wanted to punch me out, I teared up as we drove away from the scene. Seeing through the rear-view mirror that I, too, was upset over the situation, Carl apologized to me. Although I didn't expect an apology, the fact that Carl responded to my feelings told me that we cared about each other.

Establishment of the Club Identity

Movement away from their gang identity meant movement toward something else, but what was the "something else" going to be? Through involvement with AFY, the kids were open to creating a formal youth club. Four distinct steps led to the establishment of the group's club identity:

1. SELECTING A CLUB NAME. The kids wanted to select a name that would reflect something that they all held in common. They tossed around names such as Filipino Youth Club, Kalihi Valley Boys, Kalihi Teen Club, and Teens for Peace. Eventually, they held a meeting and voted on Kalihi Youth Club for their club's name.
2. CREATING A CLUB LOGO. A few group sessions were held to develop ideas for a club logo. The group unanimously selected the peace symbol for their logo and decided to inscribe "Increase the Peace" within the peace sign.

3. FUND-RAISING. The group sold candy and beef jerky, and they hosted car washes to raise money to cover the cost of printing T-shirts. This gave them a sense of ownership and also taught them the business aspect of producing their shirts.
4. PRINTING CLUB T-SHIRTS. A local printing company was able to silk-screen the group's design onto shirts. The group selected the color of the shirts as well as the color and size of the print and logo design.

All of the above-mentioned steps served to empower the youth in several ways. They utilized the democratic decision-making process to resolve issues related to their club, which helped them understand participatory democracy instead of the more common "might makes right." Fundraising and purchasing club shirts gave the group a practical sense of group ownership. The process also helped bring about the final transition from gang into prosocial friendship group.

BABY GANGSTERS

Young Sons of Samoa
Staff Member: McKay Schwenke, BA

The Baby Gangsters, or B.G.s, from Kuhio Park Terrace, are a gang consisting of males ranging from eleven to sixteen years of age. They are all of Samoan ethnicity.

Shortly after initiating therapeutic intervention two years ago, I characterized them in a television interview as a group of "young, untamed rebels who thrived on cheap thrills such as vandalism, stealing, fighting, and mobbing, and whose quenchless appetite for causing trouble occasionally set off violence on campuses of schools they attended." The acts they committed were terroristic threatening, hijacking, theft, breaking and entering, property damage (including vandalism and graffiti), truancy, and intimidating students and teachers alike. This behavior was intended to reinforce their "fearless reputation." Many who feared them became ultimate victims, primarily students their own age and younger, who were overpowered and unable to fend for themselves.

Local police officers in the Kalihi District were accustomed to arresting members of this gang on a regular basis. The consequences for committing these violations were either confinement in the youth detention center or community service within their own community. The work entailed picking up trash, cutting grass, weeding, and basically cleaning up in general. No manner of punishment appeared successful, and their antisocial behaviors continued to be repeated over and over again. After being disciplined by the law, they would immediately revert to committing crimes. It was a game of cat and mouse—them against the system. The more they got caught, the more challenging it became to deceive and elude authorities. It seemed as though these youths had no remorse for their actions—at least not until AFY intervened. However, subsequently, the B.G.s were determined to bury the past and look ahead toward a productive future.

This case study of the Baby Gangsters will describe how prevention and intervention therapy through AFY brought about positive changes by applying several fundamental principles of Redirectional Therapy. But first, a brief explanation of how I originally met the gang and the relationship and rapport that emerged.

I met the B.G.s through my association with older gang members who belonged to two other gangs, the "Peewees," and the "Junior SOS," also from Kuhio Park Terrace. At the time, I was assisting Simi Hingano, a fellow staff member, who also happened to be the outreach worker assigned to the two gangs. During our weekly visits to Kuhio Park Terrace, I consistently noticed a grouping of youths who regularly congregated outside the neighborhood community center. The Peewees referred to them as "menaces" and "trouble makers" with a reputation for stealing. They added that many of them were truant from school and would hide out in the community from police officers and school officials. I approached a couple of the group's members to set up a possible meeting time with the entire group. Two days later the meeting was held, with approximately fourteen members present. During the course of our discussion, I enlightened them on what my role as a friend and social worker would be. Later, I sat and listened as they candidly shared background information about themselves, individually, and about the gang. I was surprised at how freely they spoke and how comfortable they felt considering this was our first official meeting together. It was as though no barriers existed between us even though we were strangers.

As I reflect back, I realize that this meeting was the genesis of a special relationship and mutuality that still exists today, even though they are now adults. The group progressed immensely in maturity, but most importantly in learning responsibility. In the process of exploring positive alternatives and avenues in the social, recreation and sports, education, employment, cultural values, and community service spheres, the boys gained meaningful experiences and expanded their horizons of the world around them. This combination of activities was applied over the course of two years to help achieve meaningful change. The following describes how I've utilized the Six-Point Plan with the B.G.s.

Culture

Awareness of our own culture and history helps us to understand who we are and where we come from and can contribute to a sense of pride and respect. Unfortunately, while most, if not all, of the B.G.'s parents are fluent in the Samoan language and culture, most of the boys who were born and raised in Hawaii appeared to be alienated from it and even ashamed. In an effort to help them gain a sense of pride in their heritage, I set out to familiarize them with their background by introducing them to Samoan songs and dances. Once this process started, it became evident that other community kids wanted to jump on the bandwagon and learn these exciting dances as well. The response to my "class" was overwhelming. It was like watching a group of little kids become ecstatic over a new and favorite toy. The culture brought out a potential within them that they never knew existed. In fact, very few people had ever seen this side of them, including their parents. To say that the parents were surprised, shocked, and amazed would not adequately describe the pleasure they experienced when they witnessed, for the first time, their sons performing at a community talent show. The community center was packed, standing room only, and the boys received a thunderous greeting of applause and yells when they entered the stage. Everyone was squeezed in like sardines, and the anticipation was overwhelming. After the talent show, many of the parents commented on how proud they were to see their sons involved in the culture. The performance brought a tear to more than one eye.

Social

In the past I've taken the B.G.s to a variety of different social events. However, the one that stands out clearly in my mind is an AFY fund-raiser at the Sheraton-Waikiki Hotel, to which the boys were invited. They were overwhelmed, to say the least, when they received the invitation to be guests of the agency. For most, it was their first time to even see the inside of an incredible hotel. In addition to being guests, they were also asked to perform on stage for an estimated seven hundred people. The preparations that led up to this evening generated a lot of excitement and enthusiasm. They felt especially honored and privileged when they were informed that the tickets were selling for $100 per person. I let them know that, indeed, I thought they were very special and deserving of this honor. To see the excitement light up their faces was truly a sight to behold. In fact, many were so excited that they went out and rented tuxedos for the evening.

That night the boys looked immaculate and handsome in their colorful dance costumes. Seeing them in their dress attire, as well, was even more spectacular because it somehow brought out the very best in their characters and personalities. Parents, who only knew their children as troublemakers and burdens, were proud of them and proud of themselves as well. (This experience demonstrated the therapeutic benefits achieved for parents when their children do well.) Their manners and overall conduct were nothing short of perfection. Some mingled with the guests. They were happy to answer questions. Even today, they often reflect back on this experience, remembering the fun they had, the people they met, and the changes that impacted their lives.

Recreation and Sports

Some of the excursions and activities that I've taken the B.G.s on have included hikes in the vicinity of the Pali Lookout, Sandy Beach, and around Kapena Falls. We have also played basketball, touch football, and less structured games, such as "bullrush," and a modified version of "Aussie rules," on a regular basis. The boys thoroughly enjoy these games because they provide the opportunity to compete individually and as a team. Games provide a healthy outlet when the adrenaline starts to flow.

I use these activities as a means for releasing much of the tension and energy these kids have—not to mention the fact that it's also healthy for them. Furthermore, I believe it helps to bring out the best in whatever they set out to accomplish in terms of effort and performance. These physical activities also provide a positive outlet for their frustrations.

Education

Before I began working with these boys, they were ditching school for a variety of reasons. Since I began working with them, I have, on numerous occasions, emphasized the importance of school and education—to think not only of the present, but of the future. I've expressed the belief that the freedom to choose among career opportunities after high school begins with obtaining a diploma. For many of the B.G.s, looking ahead to their senior year in high school seemed like looking well into the future, and some found it difficult to plan for something that seemed so distant. I helped them with short-range goals such as attending school daily, being prompt to school and classes, staying out of trouble both on campus and off, and making an effort in their respective classes to improve semester grades. Through 1994 and 1995 attendance and grades improved significantly. In June 1995 we experienced our first class of graduates.

Employment and Careers

From time to time, I assisted the boys in finding employment. I showed them how to fill out application forms and how to locate job vacancies. The first summer, I was informed by one of the Kuhio Park Terrace tenants' officials that they were looking for about fourteen youths to help with repair work in the community. The group immediately responded and were quickly called in for interviews and later were accepted to fill the available openings. They were excited about earning paychecks and receiving money for themselves rather than pestering their parents.

Community Service

The boys and I experienced several community service projects, all of which were fun and memorable. However, the graffiti paint-out that we took part in was a highlight. With the help of the Community Policing Program, which generously donated the paint, rollers, and paint brushes, we were able to organize a major service project. Over sixty youths, representing different SOS generations, showed up to help paint out graffiti that was scribbled on the exterior walls of two of the main stores located at the entrance to the KPT housing project. The graffiti was placed there by none other than the boys themselves. This project was an excellent opportunity for the boys to give something back to their community. For several years afterwards the stores remained graffiti-free. It demonstrated that these kids were starting to take pride in their community and were willing to put forth the effort to sustain and maintain a safe, beautiful, and serene environment. The event also generated new respect for AFY by the police. They, for the first time, recognized the impact that AFY had on the groups. They had expected only a handful of kids, if that, to show up. When this small army appeared they were amazed.

Style and Approach

As an outreach worker, I've always tried to provide a listening ear, whether dealing with individual or collective problems. As problems crop up, I immediately try to address them openly and in a democratic way. I realize that changes won't occur overnight, but I believe, that with a lot of love and patience, the lives of these boys can be affected forever. Weaknesses and imperfections are, of course, still evident, but not to the degree and extent that once prevailed. I am very open to their concerns and try to explore various alternatives as they strive to change. It's important to be flexible and to not be weighed down with a set curriculum. If one problem-solving approach doesn't work, then I quickly resort to something else. Being creative, open-minded, nonjudgmental, and honest, have all contributed to the major changes that have empowered these kids. They have graciously taken me in as part of their close-knit family, because I have also treated them like family. The outcome has been mutual respect. I believe, also, that as our relationship grew and strengthened, their ability to comprehend and appreciate the potentiality for a better and healthier life was also established.

One of the great lessons these boys learned was that there was no need to engage in stealing, robbing, and assaulting to gain respect or build a reputation. Instead, they found that respect could be earned by serving the community. They are now remembered by their good works and service rather than by their criminal records.

Chapter 8

A Prescription of Hope

Adult Friends for Youth has presented Redirectional Therapy (RT) as a prescription of hope for significantly reducing the perplexing youth gang problem, based on almost twenty-five years of experience. It has learned how to access youth in this population, gain their trust, and help them develop feelings of competency that prepare them to become functional and healthy members of society.

It has presented youth gangs as, primarily, a group phenomenon of low-income and mostly minority youth, and takes the view that change from destructive to constructive behaviors is therapeutically achievable for most gang members. It believes that the concepts embedded in RT are the missing links for achieving prosocial change with this population.

RT requires the presence of certain elements for success. Among them is the willingness for communities to commit resources for a lengthy period of time. With time—three to four years for each group is the average—change will take root. Of course noticeable changes will also be occurring throughout this period. The best news is that several groups can be helped simultaneously, so that over a three-to-four-year time frame an entire community may likely find itself relatively free of gangs. On one hand, it can be predicted that, at minimum, the gang problem will be manageable. On the other hand, we have found that change can be extraordinary. Whole gangs have evolved into socially acceptable friendship groups, and whole neighborhoods have become relatively gang-free.

Service at a less-intense maintenance level, with groups and individuals, may be required to prevent subsequent generations from becoming gang involved. There is no silver bullet. Communities and schools that are serious about resolving problems with gangs and troubled youth must be in it for the long haul. The results, in AFY's experience, have been transformational, both economically and socially.

Another element to success is the willingness of government agencies, principal among them being the Office of Juvenile Justice and Delinquency Prevention (OJJDP), to relinquish the position that law enforcement must be part of every service directed at youth gangs. Success with the high-risk/gang population depends on absolute trust. The slightest hint that there is collusion with law enforcement, or any other entity for that matter, undermines that trust, and, thereby, the therapeutic relationship. Cooperative relationships, therefore, must be selective and transparent, and, in effect, be approved by the group.

An OJJDP report (Howell, p. 55) concluded, ". . .The complexity of the youth gang problem defies an easy solution or single strategy. Current knowledge about which programs are effective in preventing and reducing youth gang problems is limited. The most effective program model will likely prove to be a combination of prevention, intervention, and suppression strategies integrated in a collaborative approach. . ."

The disappointment with OJJDP is that, in spite of its own conclusion that there is no evidence that anything works in changing the behavior of youth gangs, it continues to cling to failed ideas such as suppression and collaboration, which give the impression of doing something while doing very little at all. For example, there continues to be an overwhelming emphasis on collaboration, when in its own report, there is only wild speculation that collaboration is effective. Also, its position that a "single strategy" can't work is more myth than reality. It's a case of repeating the same tired concepts over and over until they become truths. Collaboration, in and of itself, sometimes appears to be a higher priority than successful change with gangs.

Government mental health programs must also adjust the way they think. As was pointed out earlier, gang kids aren't going to be reached by first counseling with parents, who often are harder to reach than their kids. The top-down philosophy, from AFY's perspective, doesn't work. Evidence is the simple fact that traditional mental health services don't reach gang youth. Many mental health professionals have acknowledged that they don't know how, nor is this something that they are motivated to do. The problem appears to lie with policy makers who are afraid of the unknown and committed to the familiar.

RT is the new kid on the block and we are convinced that it does work. The stories of our clients, twelve which we have shared, support our hypothesis. Short of a scientific, controlled, longitudinal study that will take years, cost millions, and, therefore, will probably never happen, it is all we have, but we believe, for now, it is enough.

Unbelievably, as this is being written, Cliff walked into the office, and handed out greeting cards to staff. His picture, taken at the AFY fundraiser where he was honored with a Young Person of the Year Award, graced the cover. Inside, he wrote:

"AFY Ohana (family),

Thank you for all your support throughout all the years."

It is only fitting that a client should write the end to this book.

Bibliography

Alinsky. Saul D. *Rules for Radicals*. New York: Vintage Books, 1972.

Belkin, Gary S. *Contemporary Psychotherapies*. 2nd ed. Monterey, California: Brooks/Cole, 1987.

Berne, Eric. *Games People Play*. New York: Grove Press, 1964.

Caday, Lawrence. "This Year I Have a Chance to Graduate." *Sunday Star-Bulletin and Advertiser*, February 14, 1993.

Cartwright, Dorwin and Alvin Zander. *Group Dynamics: Research and Theory*. New York: Harper & Row. 1968.

Catterall, Lee. "Police Perceived as 'a Gang Too' in Crackdowns." *Honolulu Star Bulletin*, July 5, 1991.

Cloward, Richard A., and Lloyd B. Ohlin. *Delinquency and Opportunity: A Theory of Delinquent Gangs*. New York: Free Press, 1960.

Corey, Gerald. *Theory and Practice of Group Counseling*. Pacific Grove, California: Brooks/Cole, 1990.

Dawley, David. *A Nation of Lords*. Prospect Heights, Illinois: Waveland Press, 1992.

Festinger, Leon H. "Informal Social Communication." *Psychological Review*, 1950.

Forsyth, Donelson R. *An Introduction to Group Dynamics*. Monterey, California: Brooks/Cole. 1993.

Gima, Craig. "UH Works to Assure More Students Graduate." *Honolulu Star Bulletin*, March 5, 2010.

Grosser, Charles. "Class Orientation of the Indigenous Staff." In George A. Brager, and Francis P. Purcell, eds., *Community Action Against Poverty*. New Haven: College and University Press. 1967. pp. 208-216.

Hagedorn, John. *People and Folks*. Chicago. Lakeview Press. 1988.

Hingano, Pasimi. *Why Samoan Youth Join Gangs: A Comparative Study of Non-Gang and Gang Members in the Kuhio Park Terrace Housing Project (Hawaii)*. Diss., University of Hawaii, 2000.

Howell, James C. "*Youth Gang Programs and Strategies*." Office of Juvenile Justice and Delinquency Prevention. August 2000. p. 55.

Miller, Walter B. *Delinquent Behavior: Culture and the Individual*. Washington, DC: National Education Association, 1959.

Miller, Walter B. "Why the United States Has Failed to Solve Its Youth Gang Problems.: In *Gangs in America*. C. Ronald Huff (ed.). Newbury Park, Calif.: Sage, 1990.

Morales, Armando T. and Bradford W. Sheafor. *Social Work: A Profession of Many Faces*. Boston: Allyn and Bacon, 1992, Chapter 15.

Napier, Rodney W. and Matti K. Gershenfeld. *Groups Theory and Experience*. Boston: Houghton Mifflin Company, 1985.

Rogers, Carl R. "The Interpersonal Relationship: The Core of Guidance." *Harvard Educational Review*, 1962, 416-429.

Rosen, Sidney M., Pasimi Hingano and Deborah Spencer. *Toward A Gang Solution. The Redirectional Method*. National Resource Center for Youth Services. University of Oklahoma, Tulsa, 1996.

Sarri, Rosemary C. "Is Social Work Inherently Conservative—Designed to Protect the Vested Interest of Dominant Power Groups?: Yes." In *Controversial Issues in Social Work*. Eileen Gambrilland, Robert Pruger (eds.). Boston: Allyn and Bacon. 1992.

Shaw, Marvin E. *Group Dynamics: The Psychology of Small Group Behavior*. New York: McGraw Hill Book Company, 1971.

Spergel, Irving A. "*Youth Gangs: An Essay Review*," Social Service Review. March 1992.

Sutherland, Edwin H., and Donald R. Cressey. *Principles of Criminology*. 5th ed. Chicago: J.B. Lippincott, 1955.

Thibaut, J.W. and H.H. Kelley. *The Social Psychology of Groups*. New York: Wiley, 1959.

Thrasher, Frederic. *The Gang. A Study of 1303 Gangs in Chicago.* Chicago: University of Chicago Press. 1928.

Yablonsky, Lewis. *The Violent Gang.* New York: Macmillan, 1962.

Weissman, Harold (ed.). *Community Development in the Mobilization for Youth.* New York: Association Press, 1969.

About Adult Friends for Youth

Adult Friends for Youth (AFY) was founded by Dr. Sid Rosen through a federal demonstration grant at the University of Hawaii School of Social Work. The grant ran from late 1985 to late 1987. AFY was incorporated as a private non-profit organization under the name Hawaii Youth Services Volunteer Program on December 8, 1986. This was the means adopted to keep the work of the organization going after the grant ended. It became independent of the University when the grant ended. The name was changed to Adult Friends for Youth in 1988.

By 1996, the same year that AFY's book *Toward a Gang Solution: The Redirectional Method* was published, the agency completed its evolution from a volunteer mentoring program for high-risk adolescents to a fully staffed professional mental health group therapy program with its own therapeutic methodology. The move toward a professional therapy program was initiated when it was concluded, despite the popular view, that volunteer mentors were ill equipped to work with this population and especially to work with gangs and other high-risk groups.

AFY is a one-of-a-kind organization that would very much like to have some peers. Unfortunately, more often than not, the population with which it works is seen as lost and so the mental health community has pretty much abandoned it. AFY's experience shows that there are great opportunities for working with these youth, and it is hopeful that this book can provide encouragement for jumping into the water.

In addition to its clinical gang and school therapy work that reaches about 450 youth weekly, AFY conducts an annual state-wide Student Transition Convention on four islands that facilitates the transition of fifth- and sixth-grade students from elementary to middle and intermediate school and from childhood to adolescence. Typically, 6,000 to 10,000 students participate annually. We also conduct an alternative school for 20 dropouts that is taught by clinical staff under the authority of the Hawaii Department of Education Adult Education Program, and an annual spring international seven-a-side youth rugby tournament with more than 200 players competing.

AFY is currently staffed by six full-time clinicians, a part-time grant writer, a part-time advisor/consultant, and two nonclinical program, administrative, and fund-raising staff.

About the Authors

The photo from top to bottom represents four generations of AFY: Authors Sid Rosen, MSW, PhD, Founder and President Emeritus and Debbie L.K. Spencer-Chun, MSW President and CEO with Malakai Maumalanga, MSW, Clinical Director; and Onolina Taotofi, Taft Junior College Student, volleyball player, and recent Farrington High School graduate.

Deborah L.K. Spencer-Chun, MSW has lived in Hawaii her entire life and with her rich cultural and ethnic heritage is truly a "keiki o ka aina" (child of the land). She is the second child of John "Didi" and Rosie Spencer. While she and husband Sean have no children by birth, Deb has hundreds of kids with whom she has worked over two decades, and has become "godmother" to many of their children. She graduated from Farrington High School where much of Adult Friends for Youth's current work with gangs is conducted.

Sidney M. Rosen, MSW, PhD is a product of Wayne State University in Detroit (BA and MSW) and the University of Hawaii (PhD). He describes his professional career before AFY as "restless." He was a gang worker and settlement house executive in Detroit before migrating to Hawaii in 1968. For the next 27 years he taught social work, helped form the faculty union, served as acting academic planner for UH, and took time off to serve as special assistant in foreign relations and defense to U.S. Senator Spark M. Matsunaga. While in Washington, D.C. he had a front row seat to the Egypt-Israel Peace Accords; the Iranian Hostage Crises, organizing a meeting between Iran's Charge D'Affaires Ali Agah and several senators; and helped start the ball rolling toward the creation of the United States Institute of Peace. He reflected that, pre-AFY, it was one of the most exciting years of his life. He has been married to Judie for 51 years, has two sons and three remarkable grandchildren.

Sid is old school and Deb says she is old school at heart. Both emerged from the field of social work practice with children and youth in different eras.

Sid was Deb's professor at the University of Hawaii School of Social Work. When he started what was to become Adult Friends for Youth, he brought her along as an intern. She never left and succeeded Sid as President and Chief Executive Officer when he retired in 2007.

Turning It Around: Redirectional Therapy, completed in conjunction with AFY's 25th Anniversary, is their second book collaboration.

CPSIA information can be obtained at www.ICGtesting.com
Printed in the USA
270432BV00001B/1/P

9 780533 164905